**TEACHER'S PET PUBLICATIONS**

LITPLAN TEACHER PACK
for
From the Mixed-up Files of
Mrs. Basil E. Frankweiler
based on the book by
E. L. Konigsburg

Written by
Catherine Caldwell & Mary B. Collins

© 2007 Teacher's Pet Publications
All Rights Reserved

COPYRIGHT 2007
Teacher's Pet Publications, Inc.

Only the student materials may be reproduced
multiple times for use in the purchaser's classroom.

For copyright questions, contact
Teacher's Pet Publications

www.tpet.com

TABLE OF CONTENTS
From the Mixed-Up Files of Mrs. Basil E. Frankweiler

Introduction	7
Unit Objectives	9
Reading Assignment Sheet	10
Unit Outline	11
Short Answer Study Questions	15
Multiple Choice Study/Quiz Questions	25
Vocabulary Worksheets	41
Lesson One	63
Non-fiction Assignment Sheet	77
Oral Reading Evaluation	74
Writing Assignment 1	80
Writing Assignment 2	89
Writing Assignment 3	96
Writing Evaluation Form	83
Vocabulary Review Ideas	98
Critical Thinking Questions	92
Unit Review Ideas	99
Unit Tests	103
Unit Resource Materials	147
Vocabulary Resource Materials	169

A FEW NOTES ABOUT THE AUTHOR
E. L. Konigsburg

"I knew I had been right about the spirit of adventure shared by good readers. I owe children a good story."

-Elaine Lobl Konigsburg

Elaine Lobl was born on February 20, 1930 in New York City. Early in her childhood, her family moved to small-town Pennsylvania, where Elaine graduated first in her high school class and became the first person from her family to attend college. The young woman earned a degree in chemistry from Carnegie Mellon, though graduate work at the University of Pittsburgh convinced her that she did not have the heart for further pursuit of the science. After she and her husband married, they moved to Florida, and Konigsburg began teaching science at a girls' school.

Through teaching young women, Konigsburg realized that she was more fascinated by the students she taught than the subject matter she presented. She left the classroom after a short time in order to raise her three children–Paul, Laurie, and Ross-- but continued to marvel at young people and their experiences in the world. While she was home raising her children, Konigsburg began taking art classes, as well. She discovered a natural talent for art, and several of her novels feature her original illustrations. Konigsburg's first novel *Jennifer, Hecate, Macbeth, William McKinley, and me, Elizabeth* won Newbery Honors in 1967, and it was followed by *From the Mixed-Up Files of Mrs. Basil E. Frankweiler*, which won the Newbery Medal in 1968. Over the next thirty years, Konigsburg would write over fifteen novels, including *The View From Saturday*, which earned her a second Newbery Medal in 1997.

INTRODUCTION
From the Mixed-Up Files of Mrs. Basil E. Frankweiler

This unit has been designed to develop students' reading, writing, thinking, and language skills through exercises and activities related to *From the Mixed-Up Files of Mrs. Basil E. Frankweiler*. It includes 22 lessons supported by extra resource materials.

In the introductory lesson students look at several interesting, old items and write short stories about the articles of their choice. Students are also introduced to the idea of the Hero's Journey. Following the introductory activity, students are given a transition to explain how the activities relate to the unit. The class will then be given materials relevant to the unit.

The reading assignments are from ten to twenty pages each; some are a little shorter while others are a little longer. Students have approximately fifteen minutes of pre-reading work to do prior to each reading assignment. This pre-reading work involves reviewing the study questions for the assignment and doing some vocabulary work for 8 to 10 vocabulary words they will encounter in their reading.

The study questions are fact-based so students can find the answers right in the text. These questions come in two formats: short answer and multiple choice. The best use of these materials is probably to use the short answer version of the questions as study guides for students (since the answers will be more complete) and to use the multiple choice version for occasional quizzes.

The vocabulary work is intended to enrich students' vocabularies as well as to aid in their understanding of the book. Prior to each reading assignment students will complete a two-part worksheet for approximately 8-10 vocabulary words in the upcoming reading assignment. Part I focuses on students' use of general knowledge and contextual clues by giving the sentence in which the word appears in the text. Students are then to write down what they think the words mean based on the words' usage. Part II nails down the definitions of the words by giving students dictionary definitions of the words and having them match the words to the correct definitions based on the words' contextual usage. Students should then have an understanding of the words when they meet them in the text.

After each reading assignment, students will go back and formulate answers for the study guide questions. Discussion of these questions serves as a review of the most important events and ideas presented in the reading assignments.

After students complete reading the work, there is a vocabulary review lesson which pulls together all of the fragmented vocabulary lists for the reading assignments and gives students a review of all the words they have studied.

Following the vocabulary review, a lesson is devoted to the critical thinking questions. These questions focus on interpretation, critical analysis, and personal responses, employing a variety of thinking skills and adding to the students' understanding of the work.

There is a group theme project in this unit. Students will divide into pairs based upon a common investigative interest. Each pair will research a particular aspect of art or history that they select, thereby becoming the class expert on that topic. Each group will then develop an original product based on their study. A presentation day is scheduled in the unit so that students may benefit from one another's work and practice their public speaking skills.

There are three writing assignments in this unit, each with the purpose of informing, persuading, or expressing personal opinions. The detailed writing assignment sheets guide students through the assignments. The first assignment is to give a personal response to an article in *The New York Times*. In the second assignment students inform Claudia (via letter) about plans they are making and ask for her advice, since she is a planning expert. In the third writing assignment, students write a letter as Mrs. Frankweiler to Mr. and Mrs. Kincaid to persuade them to be lenient on the children when they return home.

There is a non-fiction reading assignment. Each student must read nonfiction articles, books, etc., to gather information about their non-fiction topics, which are related to the book.

The review lesson pulls together all of the aspects of the unit. The teacher is given several choices of activities or games to use which all serve the same basic function of reviewing all of the information presented in the unit.

The unit test comes in two formats: short answer and multiple choice. As a convenience, two different tests for each format have been included. There is also an advanced short answer test for advanced students.

There are additional support materials included with this unit. The unit resource materials section includes suggestions for an in-class library, crossword and word search puzzles related to the book, and extra worksheets. There is a list of bulletin board ideas which gives the teacher suggestions for bulletin boards to go along with this unit. In additions, there is a list of extra class activities the teacher could choose from to enhance the unit or as a substitution for an exercise the teacher might feel is inappropriate for his/her class. Answer keys are located directly after the reproducible student materials throughout the unit. The vocabulary resource materials section includes puzzles, worksheets, and games to reinforce the vocabulary work done in the unit.

The level of this unit can be varied depending upon the criteria on which the individual assignments are graded, the teacher's expectations of the students in class discussions, and the formats chosen for the study guides, quizzes, and tests. If teachers have other ideas or activities they wish to use, they can usually easily be inserted prior to the review lesson.

The student materials may be reproduced for use in the teacher's classroom without infringement of copyrights. No other portion of this unit may be reproduced without the written consent of Teacher's Pet Publications, Inc.

UNIT OBJECTIVES
From the Mixed-Up Files of Mrs. Basil E. Frankweiler

Through reading *From the Mixed-Up Files of Mrs. Basil E. Frankweiler* students will explore themes of the novel and make connections to themselves and the larger world.

Students will demonstrate their understanding of the text of four levels: factual, interpretive, critical, and personal.

Students will gain a better knowledge of nonfiction topics presented in the novel. Students will pursue their own interests within a partnership dynamic.

Students will practice reading orally and silently to improve their reading proficiency.

Students will answer questions to demonstrate their knowledge and understanding of the main events and characters in the book as they relate to the author's theme development.

Students will enrich their vocabularies and improve their understanding of the novel through the vocabulary lessons prepared for use in conjunction with the novel.

The writing assignments in this unit are geared to several purposes:
- To have students demonstrate their abilities to inform, persuade or express their own ideas
- To check students' reading comprehension
- To make students think about the ideas presented in the book
- To encourage logical thinking
- To improve students' use of the English language

Students will read aloud, report, and participate in large and small group discussions in order to improve their public speaking and personal interaction skills.

READING ASSIGNMENT SHEET
From the Mixed-Up Files of Mrs. Basil E. Frankweiler

Date Assigned	Assignment	Completion Date
	Chapter 1	
	Chapter 2	
	Chapter 3	
	Chapter 4	
	Chapter 5	
	Chapter 6	
	Chapter 7	
	Chapter 8	
	Chapter 9	
	Chapter 10	

UNIT OUTLINE
From the Mixed-Up Files of Mrs. Basil E. Frankweiler

1 Introduction	2 Read Ch 1 Oral Rdg Eval KWL Character Chart	3 Review Ch 1 Read Ch 2 Oral Rdg Eval	4 Review Ch 2 Non-fiction Read Ch 3	5 Review Ch 3 Update KWL "Secrets" Read Ch 4
6 Review Ch 4 NY Times Writing #1 Read Ch 5	7 Review Ch 5 Read Ch 6-8	8 Read Ch 6-8	9 Quiz Ch 6-8 "Heroism" Update KWL	10 Writing #2 Read Ch 9
11 Review Ch 9 Read Ch 10	12 Review Ch 10 Non-fiction Reports	13 Extra Discussion Questions	14 Extra Discussion Questions	15 Writing #3
16 Vocabulary Review	17 Unit Review	18 Unit Test		

Key: P = Preview Study Questions   V = Vocabulary Work   R= Read

SHORT ANSWER
STUDY QUESTIONS

Mixed-Up Files **Study Questions**
Chapter 1
1. Where does Claudia plan to go when she runs away?
2. Who does Claudia choose to take with her?
3. Why does Claudia think Jamie will make a good companion?
4. Why does Claudia love New York City?
5. What is one of Claudia's special talents?
6. What discovery does Claudia consider an "invitation to leave on Wednesday"?
7. In what activity do Jamie and Bruce participate each day on the school bus?
8. What changes Jamie's attitude towards running away?
9. How does Jamie make extra money?

Chapter 2
1. Where does Jamie find his list of instructions from Claudia?
2. How do Claudia and Jamie manage to skip school?
3. Why does Jamie make so much noise when he walks?
4. Why do Jamie and Claudia argue as they get off the bus?
5. Who are the recipients of the letters Claudia mails on the day they leave home?

Chapter 3
1. What is Jamie's first decision as treasurer?
2. Why does Claudia suggest they skip Fifth Avenue?
3. How does Jamie cool Claudia's anger?
4. What is Claudia's plan for closing time at the museum on the first day?
5. What do Claudia and Jamie do until 5:30 PM on their first day at the museum?

Chapter 4
1. What is Claudia's most treasured luxury?
2. What does Claudia put in the sarcophagus?
3. What close call does Jamie have the first morning?
4. How do the children choose to spend their days at the museum?
5. What are the tourists waiting in line to see?
6. How does Claudia finally acquire a *New York Times* newspaper?
7. What do Claudia and Jamie learn about the interesting statue?
8. How does Claudia plan to focus their learning?
9. How does Jamie think they should begin their investigation of the statue?

Mixed-Up Files **Study Questions**
Chapter 5
1. What problem do Claudia and Jamie encounter after three days at the museum?
2. Why do the siblings go to 42nd Street? How do they get there?
3. How do Claudia and Jamie divide the research project?
4. What does Jamie learn from eavesdropping in the men's room?
5. Where do Claudia and Jamie find unexpected income?
6. Describe Claudia's and Jamie's discussion about homesickness.

Chapter 6
1. What does Claudia notice about the velvet that rested underneath Angel?
2. What conclusion do Claudia and Jamie draw after looking at the velvet?
3. What do the siblings decide to do about their newfound knowledge?
4. Why won't Claudia return home without discovering who created "Angel"?

Chapter 7
1. How do Claudia and Jamie justify spending so much of their money on a mailbox rental?
2. Who do the siblings run into in the mastaba?
3. How does Claudia use the encounter in the mastaba to her advantage?

Chapter 8
1. Where do the children decide to spend the majority of their day on Tuesday?
2. Why does Claudia cry when she reads the letter from the museum officials?
3. Why isn't Claudia ready to go home yet?
4. To where does Claudia want to buy tickets? Why?

Chapter 9
1. How do the children spend the last of their money?
2. Who is Parks?
3. What question does Parks ask the children?
4. Describe Mrs. Frankweiler's office.
5. Who does Mrs. Frankweiler call while the children are waiting to see her?
6. What does Mrs. Frankweiler ask Parks to bring her?
7. What secret does Jamie share with Mrs. Frankweiler?
8. Why doesn't Claudia want to tell Mrs. Frankweiler where she and Jamie stayed all week?
9. What are the terms of Mrs. Frankweiler's bargain regarding the secret of Angel?
10. What do Claudia and Jamie find in the file labeled "Bologna, Italy"?
11. Why does Claudia begin to cry?
12. What deal does Mrs. Frankweiler make with Jamie and Claudia?
13. What is the one "impossible" thing that Mrs. Frankweiler would like to experience?

Mixed-Up Files **Study Questions**
Chapter 10
1. Who wins the game of "war" between Jamie and Mrs. Frankweiler?
2. What transportation do Claudia and Jamie take back to Greenwich?
3. What discovery does Claudia make about human nature and secrets?
4. What do the children plan to do every time they save enough money?
5. How do the children plan to make Mrs. Frankweiler a grandmother without her being a mother?
6. How is Saxonberg connected to the characters in the novel?
7. What secret does Mrs. Frankweiler keep from Claudia and Jamie?

Mixed-Up Files **Study Question Answers**
Chapter 1

1. Where does Claudia plan to go when she runs away?
    She plans to go to the Metropolitan Museum of Art in New York City.

2. Who does Claudia choose to take with her?
    She chooses Jamie, the second-youngest of her three brothers.

3. Why does Claudia think Jamie will make a good companion?
    She knows he can keep quiet, will provide her with the occasional laugh, and has more money than any kid she knows.

4. Why does Claudia love New York City?
    She loved it because it was important; it was elegant; and it was busy.

5. What is one of Claudia's special talents?
    Claudia could plan long and well.

6. What discovery does Claudia consider an "invitation to leave on Wednesday"?
    Claudia finds a train pass in the wastebasket with one adult ride left on it, which would allow Claudia and Jamie to travel for free since a child's fare only costs half on an adult fare.

7. In what activity do Jamie and Bruce participate each day on the school bus?
    They play the card game "war."

8. What changes Jamie's attitude towards running away?
    He is flattered by the fact that Claudia has chosen him instead of Steve.

9. How does Jamie make extra money?
    He makes extra money by gambling at cards, playing "war" with Bruce.

Mixed-Up Files **Study Question Answers**
Chapter 2

1. Where does Jamie find his list of instructions from Claudia?
    They are under his pillow, pinned to his pajamas.

2. How do Claudia and Jamie manage to skip school?
    They stowaway on the school bus, hiding until the bus driver parks and leaves the bus unattended after his delivery to the school.

3. Why does Jamie make so much noise when he walks?
    He is carrying $24.43 in coins in his pockets.

4. Why do Jamie and Claudia argue as they get off the bus?
   Jamie assumes they will hide in the woods, which Claudia feels is ridiculous. They also argue over grammar–"hide" versus "hide out in."

5. Who are the recipients of the letters Claudia mails on the day they leave home?
   One envelope contains a letter to their parents, explaining that they have run away. The other envelope is going to the corn flakes company for a 25 cent box top rebate.

Mixed-Up Files Study Question Answers
Chapter 3

1. What is Jamie's first decision as treasurer?
   The pair will walk to the museum, rather than take a bus or a taxi.

2. Why does Claudia suggest they skip Fifth Avenue?
   She sarcastically hints that strolling down 5th Avenue might make her want to shop.

3. How does Jamie cool Claudia's anger?
   He flatters her by calling her "brilliant."

4. What is Claudia's plan for closing time at the museum on the first day?
   The siblings will go to the restrooms right before closing time and hide in the stalls–"feet up, head down, door open."

5. What do Claudia and Jamie do until 5:30 PM on their first day at the museum?
   They wander around the museum looking for a place to spend the night.

Mixed-Up Files Study Question Answers
Chapter 4

1. What is Claudia's most treasured luxury?
   Claudia treasures "good, clean smells."

2. What does Claudia put in the sarcophagus?
   She puts her violin case (which she is using as a suitcase) into the sarcophagus.

3. What close call does Jamie have the first morning?
   He believes that the running water he hears is initiated by a visitor; in fact, it is a janitor filling his bucket.

4. How do the children choose to spend their days at the museum?
   Claudia decides that they should learn everything they can about the museum.

5. What are the tourists waiting in line to see?
   They are waiting to see a statue of an angel with her arms folded, looking holy.

6. How does Claudia finally acquire a *New York Times* newspaper?
   She steals it from a man who leaves it on the counter when he goes to look at reproductions of antique jewelry.

7. What do Claudia and Jamie learn about the interesting statue?
   The statue was purchased for $225 from the collection of Mrs. Basil E. Frankweiler. The marble statue named "Angel" might be the work of Michelangelo. Frankweiler claims to have purchased the piece prior to WWII from a dealer in Bologna, Italy.

8. How does Claudia plan to focus their learning?
   She decides to focus their learning on Michelangelo and determining whether or not he actually created "Angel." She decides they will continue to learn something about everything else in the museum, as well, though not to the same extent she had initially planned.

9. How does Jamie think they should begin their investigation of the statue?
   He thinks they should examine fingerprints and attempt to match them to other works by Michelangelo.

Mixed-Up Files Study Question Answers
Chapter 5

1. What problem do Claudia and Jamie encounter after three days at the museum?
   They are running out of clean laundry.

2. Why do the siblings go to 42nd Street? How do they get there?
   They walk to the library on 42nd Street in order to conduct research about Michelangelo and the Renaissance.

3. How do Claudia and Jamie divide the research project?
   Claudia assigns Jamie the task of looking through books for pictures of "Angel," while she concentrates on reading.

4. What does Jamie learn from eavesdropping in the men's room?
   He learns that the guards are going to move "Angel" that night.

5. Where do Claudia and Jamie find unexpected income?
   They find coins in the fountain where they bathe.

6. Describe Claudia's and Jamie's discussion about homesickness.
   Claudia and Jamie attempt to discover why they are not homesick. They recall the time when they had to stay with their aunt while their mother had a baby and that they were homesick then. They come to the conclusion that they are more sure of themselves and better trained, which is why they are not homesick this time.

Mixed-Up Files Study Question Answers
Chapter 6

1. What does Claudia notice about the velvet that rested underneath Angel?
   An impression was made by the statue and memorized by the velvet–three rings with an "M" (the children suppose) in the middle of one of the rings.

2. What conclusion do Claudia and Jamie draw after looking at the velvet?
   They decide to investigate the mark further since Jamie can recall seeing the mark on one of the books during the previous day's research. They discover that the mark is Michelangelo's stonemason's mark.

3. What do the siblings decide to do about their newfound knowledge?
   They will write the Metropolitan to let them know the importance of the mark on the velvet.

4. Why won't Claudia return home without discovering who created "Angel"?
   She believes that making this discovery would allow her to go home "different."

Mixed-Up Files Study Question Answers
Chapter 7

1. How do Claudia and Jamie justify spending so much of their money on a mailbox rental?
   They can get more money by bathing in the fountain.

2. Who do the siblings run into in the mastaba?
   They run into Jamie's classmates.

3. How does Claudia use the encounter in the mastaba to her advantage?
   She is going to have Jamie deliver the letter and claim to be from the third-grade class visiting from Greenwich. He can further claim to be Bruce Lansing–"but only if they ask."

Mixed-Up Files Study Question Answers
Chapter 8

1. Where do the children decide to spend the majority of their day on Tuesday?
    They take a tour of the U. N.

2. Why does Claudia cry when she reads the letter from the museum officials?
    She doesn't know what else to do about a "polite letter of rejection." She feels they have accomplished nothing because they did not accomplish their goal of solving the mystery surrounding "Angel."

3. Why isn't Claudia ready to go home yet?
    She can't explain it, but she feels that a "real discovery will help" her return home as a changed individual.

4. To where does Claudia want to buy tickets? Why?
    She wants to go to Farmington, Connecticut to the home of Mrs. Frankweiler. Claudia hopes she will be able to find the answers she needs there.

Mixed-Up Files Study Question Answers
Chapter 9

1. How do the children spend the last of their money?
    They purchase taxi fare to Farmington from Hartford, Connecticut.

2. Who is Parks?
    Parks is Mrs. Frankweiler's butler.

3. What question does Parks ask the children?
    He asks who they are and what their business is.

4. Describe Mrs. Frankweiler's office.
    It looks much like a lab, with Formica, vinyl, steel, and fluorescent lighting. The walls, however, are lined with rows of filing cabinets.

5. Who does Mrs. Frankweiler call while the children are waiting to see her?
    She calls Saxonberg.

6. What does Mrs. Frankweiler ask Parks to bring her?
    She asks for a mirror.

7. What secret does Jamie share with Mrs. Frankweiler?
    He tells her that he and Claudia have been staying at the Metropolitan all week.

8. Why doesn't Claudia want to tell Mrs. Frankweiler where she and Jamie stayed all week?
   She wants to have a secret, just as Mrs. Frankweiler holds the secret about "Angel."

9. What are the terms of Mrs. Frankweiler's bargain regarding the secret of Angel?
   Mrs. Frankweiler gives the pair one hour to find the secret about Angel in her filing cabinets. At the end of the hour, the pair will give her the details of their week at the Met, and Frankweiler will have her driver, Sheldon, take them home.

10. What do Claudia and Jamie find in the file labeled "Bologna, Italy"?
    They find a two-sided document. On side one is written a sonnet by Michelangelo. Side two contains a sketch of Angel.

11. Why does Claudia begin to cry?
    She finally has the information that will make her "different." She also recognizes that Michelangelo held the document hundreds of years before.

12. What deal does Mrs. Frankweiler make with Jamie and Claudia?
    If they promise not to tell the secret of Angel while Mrs. Frankweiler is alive, she will bequeath the sketch to them in her will.

13. What is the one "impossible" thing that Mrs. Frankweiler would like to experience?
    She would like to be a mother.

Mixed-Up Files **Study Question Answers**
Chapter 10

1. Who wins the game of "war" between Jamie and Mrs. Frankweiler?
   Jamie wins.

2. What transportation do Claudia and Jamie take back to Greenwich?
   Sheldon drives them back in the Rolls Royce.

3. What discovery does Claudia make about human nature and secrets?
   ". . . after a time having a secret and nobody knowing you have a secret is no fun. And although you don't want others to know what the secret is, you want them to at least know you have one."

4. What do the children plan to do every time they save enough money?
   They plan to visit Mrs. Frankweiler.

5. How do the children plan to make Mrs. Frankweiler a grandmother without her being a mother?
   They plan to secretly adopt her, telling no one–not even Mrs. Frankweiler.

6. How is Saxonberg connected to the characters in the novel?
    He is Mrs. Frankweiler's attorney and Claudia's and Jamie's grandfather.

7. What secret does Mrs. Frankweiler keep from Claudia and Jamie?
    Their grandfather has been her lawyer for forty-one years.

Mixed-Up Files Multiple Choice Questions
Chapter 1

1. Where does Claudia plan to go when she runs away?
    A. Her grandparents' house
    B. Her best friend's house
    C. The Metropolitan Museum of Art
    D. The Bronx Zoo

2. Who does Claudia choose to take with her?
    A. Her best friend
    B. Her little brother
    C. Her neighbor, Jamie
    D. Her cat

3. Why does Claudia think Jamie will make a good companion?
    A. He would be able to keep quiet.
    B. He is good for a laugh every now and then.
    C. He is rich.
    D. All of the above

4. Why does Claudia love New York City?
    A. It is elegant, important, and busy.
    B. It is fun, exciting, and new.
    C. It is large, bustling, and expensive.
    D. It is far away.

5. What is one of Claudia's special talents?
    A. Dancing
    B. Playing the violin
    C. Planning
    D. Singing

6. What discovery does Claudia consider an "invitation to leave on Wednesday"?
    A. Her parents would be out of town.
    B. She found a twenty-dollar bill.
    C. She found out she was invited to a friend's birthday party.
    D. She found a train pass with funds available on it.

7. In what activity do Jamie and Bruce participate each day on the school bus?
    A. They exchange baseball cards.
    B. They play "war."
    C. They play checkers.
    D. They play "I spy."

Mixed-Up Files **Multiple Choice Questions**
Chapter 1 Continued

8. What changes Jamie's attitude towards running away?
    A. He is flattered that Claudia chose him for a partner.
    B. Claudia promises him a lot of money.
    C. He gets in trouble at school.
    D. He has a fight with his best friend.

9. How does Jamie make extra money?
    A. He walks the neighborhood dogs.
    B. He mows grass.
    C. He works for his grandfather.
    D. He gambles playing cards.

Mixed-Up Files **Multiple Choice Questions**
Chapter 2

1. Where does Jamie find his list of instructions from Claudia?
    A. On the bathroom mirror
    B. Under his pillow
    C. Taped to his bicycle
    D. In his spelling book

2. How do Claudia and Jamie manage to skip school?
    A. They pretend to be sick and stay home.
    B. They hide in the principal's office.
    C. They hide on the bus.
    D. They slip out at recess.

3. Why does Jamie make so much noise when he walks?
    A. His wet tennis shoes squeak.
    B. He has hard-soled shoes.
    C. He is carrying over twenty dollars in change.
    D. He has a tack stuck in the bottom of his shoe.

4. Why do Jamie and Claudia argue as they get off the bus?
    A. They argue about where they will hide.
    B. They argue about where to eat lunch.
    C. They argue about the best baseball team.
    D. They argue about how far they are from home.

5. Who are the recipients of the letters Claudia mails on the day they leave home?
    A. The President and the FBI
    B. Claudia's and Jamie's best friends
    C. Her parents and a cereal company
    D. Her parents and The Metropolitan Museum

Mixed-Up Files **Multiple Choice Questions**
Chapter 3

1. What is Jamie's first decision as treasurer?
    A. To walk to the museum
    B. To change their money into larger bills
    C. To eat only cereal for the entire trip
    D. To stay in a hotel

2. Why does Claudia suggest they skip Fifth Avenue?
    A. She is afraid.
    B. She is tired.
    C. She would be tempted to buy things.
    D. It is too far out of their way.

3. How does Jamie cool Claudia's anger?
    A. He tells her she is brilliant.
    B. He gives her a piece of chocolate.
    C. He calls a taxi for her.
    D. He gives her a hug.

4. What is Claudia's plan for closing time at the museum on the first day?
    A. Leave through the front door and re-enter through the back
    B. Call their parents to come get them
    C. Leave with one of the families in the museum
    D. Climb into the sarcophagus

5. What do Claudia and Jamie do until 5:30 PM on their first day at the museum?
    A. Eat hot dogs from a street vendor
    B. Walk up and down Fifth Avenue
    C. Hide in the restrooms
    D. Hide behind a large statue in the lobby

Mixed-Up Files **Multiple Choice Questions**
Chapter 4
1. What is Claudia's most treasured luxury?
    A. Good, clean smells
    B. Flannel sheets
    C. Nail polish
    D. Chocolate

2. What does Claudia put in the sarcophagus?
    A. Her purse
    B. A suitcase
    C. Her lunch
    D. The violin case

3. What close call does Jamie have the first morning?
    A. His mother almost sees him in front of the museum.
    B. He almost gets caught stealing.
    C. The janitor finds him in the bathroom.
    D. He almost falls down a flight of stairs.

4. How do the children choose to spend their days at the museum?
    A. They plan to sit in the snack bar and watch people go by.
    B. They plan to learn as much as they can about one gallery per day.
    C. They plan to create a map of the museum so they can find their way around.
    D. They plan to draw pictures of their favorite rooms in the museum.

5. What are the tourists waiting in line to see?
    A. A King Tut exhibit
    B. *The Nutcracker*
    C. *Mona Lisa*
    D. A statue that looks like an angel

6. How does Claudia finally acquire a *New York Times* newspaper?
    A. A woman unexpectedly offers one to her.
    B. She buys one.
    C. She takes one off the counter when a man leaves it unattended.
    D. She asks to borrow one from one of the coffee shop customers.

7. What do Claudia and Jamie learn about the interesting statue?
    A. It was created by a professor at a local college.
    B. It was created by two six-year-old girls from Syracuse.
    C. It is solid gold.
    D. It might have been created by Michelangelo.

Mixed-Up Files **Multiple Choice Questions**
Chapter 4 Continued

8. How does Claudia plan to focus their learning at the museum?
    A. They will choose one painting from one gallery each day.
    B. They will learn about the museum's featured item each day.
    C. They will focus on Michelangelo and "Angel."
    D. They will follow a tour brochure they found.

9. How does Jamie think they should begin their investigation of the statue?
    A. By taking a lot of pictures of the statue and studying them
    B. By looking at books about Michelangelo
    C. By examining the signature on the bottom of the statue
    D. By looking for Michelangelo's fingerprints on the statue

Mixed-Up Files **Multiple Choice Questions**
Chapter 5
1. What problem do Claudia and Jamie encounter after three days at the museum?
    A. They run out of money.
    B. They run out of food.
    C. They run out of energy.
    D. They run out of clean clothes.

2. Why do the siblings go to 42nd Street?
    A. To conduct research at the library
    B. To shop
    C. To eat lunch
    D. To visit Mrs. Frankweiler

3. How do Claudia and Jamie divide the research project?
    A. Claudia looks for books; Jamie checks the Internet
    B. Claudia looks in A-M; Jamie looks in N-Z.
    C. Claudia looks up Michelangelo; Jamie looks up Angel.
    D. Claudia reads reference books; Jamie looks in picture books.

4. What does Jamie learn from eavesdropping in the men's room?
    A. The Metropolitan will be closed on Sunday.
    B. Angel is going to be moved to a new location in the museum.
    C. Angel is a fake.
    D. The janitors suspect children are living in the museum.

5. Where do Claudia and Jamie find unexpected income?
    A. Tip money left for waitresses in the snack bar
    B. Change left behind at the vending machines
    C. A lost wallet in the restroom
    D. Coins in their bathing fountain

6. Describe Claudia's and Jamie's discussion about homesickness.
    A. Claudia tells Jamie to be more "grown up," that homesickness is for babies.
    B. Jamie and Claudia are both homesick and decide that they should go home soon.
    C. They decide they're not homesick because they are more sure of themselves and better trained.
    D. Claudia is too busy to be homesick; she really wants to find out about Michelangelo. Jamie, on the other hand, is very homesick and wishes she would just give up and go home.

Mixed-Up Files **Multiple Choice Questions**
Chapter 6
1. What does Claudia notice about the velvet that rested underneath Angel?
    A. It looks just like her curtains at home.
    B. It is not really velvet.
    C. It is marked by an impression from the bottom of the statue.
    D. It is her favorite color.

2. What conclusion do Claudia and Jamie draw after looking at the velvet?
    A. It was originally commissioned for an Olympic event.
    B. It was stolen.
    C. It was created by Michelangelo.
    D. It was created by someone whose name began with "W."

3. What do the siblings decide to do about their new knowledge?
    A. Write an article for the newspaper explaining their findings.
    B. Write a letter to the museum explaining their findings.
    C. Write a letter to their parents explaining their findings.
    D. Save the information for some later time when it would be more useful.

4. Why won't Claudia return home without discovering who created "Angel"?
    A. She won't be any "different" if they don't find out about Angel.
    B. The whole reason for leaving home was to find out about Angel; she doesn't want to go until her mission is accomplished.
    C. If they solve the riddle, their leaving home and breaking the museum rules might be forgiven.
    D. She wants to collect the reward money for solving the mystery.

Mixed-Up Files Multiple Choice Questions
Chapter 7

1. How do Claudia and Jamie justify spending so much of their money on a mailbox rental?
    A. They can replace the funds.
    B. They are going home the next day.
    C. They are expecting a large sum of money to be sent to the mailbox.
    D. They use money from the wallet they found.

2. Who do the siblings run into in the mastaba?
    A. Their mother
    B. The security guards
    C. Jamie's classmates
    D. A janitor

3. How does Claudia use the encounter in the mastaba to her advantage?
    A. She finds a good place to hide.
    B. She overhears two knowledgeable museum patrons talking about Angel.
    C. She is able to have Jamie deliver a letter to the museum officials without giving away his identity.
    D. She gets some of Jamie's friends to sneak them some food.

Mixed-Up Files **Multiple Choice Questions**
Chapter 8
1. Where do the children decide to spend the majority of their day on Tuesday?
    A. Researching Angel
    B. Resting
    C. Studying in the museum
    D. Touring the U.N.

2. Why does Claudia cry when she reads the letter from the museum officials?
    A. The letter of rejection is so polite that she can't be angry; just sad.
    B. The letter tells how worried her parents are.
    C. The letter tells that Angel is being moved to a different museum.
    D. The letter says the mystery has already been solved.

3. Why isn't Claudia ready to go home yet?
    A. She hasn't heard from her parents.
    B. She hasn't seen enough of the city on her own.
    C. She hasn't accomplished anything.
    D. She hasn't gotten over being angry.

4. To where does Claudia want to buy tickets?
    A. Italy
    B. Farmington, CT
    C. Home
    D. New York

Mixed-Up Files **Multiple Choice Questions**
Chapter 9
1. How do the children spend the last of their money?
    A. Lunch
    B. Taxi fare and tip
    C. Newspaper
    D. Bus fare

2. Who is Parks?
    A. Museum security guard
    B. Mrs. Frankweiler's chauffeur
    C. Claudia's grandfather
    D. Mrs. Frankweiler's butler

3. What question does Parks ask the children?
    A. Who they are
    B. How old they are
    C. The name of their school
    D. All of the above

4. Describe Mrs. Frankweiler's office.
    A. It looks like a lab but with filing cabinets lining the walls.
    B. It looks like a bank with a big vault.
    C. It looks like an old-time general store.
    D. It looks like a museum.

5. Who does Mrs. Frankweiler call while the children are waiting to see her?
    A. The police
    B. Saxonberg
    C. The children's parents
    D. The museum

6. What does Mrs. Frankweiler ask Parks to bring her?
    A. A mirror
    B. A file
    C. A drawing of Angel
    D. The car

7. What secret does Jamie Share with Mrs. Frankweiler?
    A. That he and Claudia have been staying at the Metropolitan Museum
    B. That Angel has Michelangelo's stonemason's mark on the bottom
    C. His method of cheating at cards
    D. That he and Claudia have been taking money from the fountain

Mixed-Up Files **Multiple Choice Questions**
Chapter 9 Continued

8. Why doesn't Claudia want to tell Mrs. Frankweiler where she and Jamie stayed all week?
    A. She wants to keep her secret.
    B. She wants to keep her bargaining power.
    C. She is afraid that telling will mean her trip is over.
    D. All of the above.

9. What are the terms of Mrs. Frankweiler's bargain regarding the secret of Angel?
    A. She will tell them the secret of Angel if the children will help her get Angel back.
    B. She will give the children 1 hour to find Angel's secret, and they will tell her the details of their week.
    C. She will tell them the secret of Angel if they will come and visit her whenever they can.
    D. She will give the children 1 hour to find the secret of Angel, but then she will call the police to take them home.

10. What do Claudia and Jamie find in the file labeled "Bologna, Italy"?
    A. The history of the first bologna sandwich
    B. Money
    C. Italian notes with Michelangelo's signature on them.
    D. Proof that Michelangelo did create Angel

11. Why does Claudia begin to cry?
    A. She is happy the mystery is solved.
    B. She finally has the information that will make her "different."
    C. She recognizes Michelangelo held the documents hundreds of years ago.
    D. All of the above

12. What deal does Mrs. Frankweiler make with Jamie and Claudia?
    A. She will bequeath the proof of Angel's background to the children if they will keep it a secret until after she dies.
    B. If she can beat Jamie at "war," she will tell them the truth about Angel.
    C. She'll tell them a secret about their grandfather if they will keep her secret about Angel.
    D. She won't turn them in to the police if they will keep her secret.

13. What is the one "impossible" thing that Mrs. Frankweiler would like to experience?
    A. Space flight
    B. A chance to talk with Michelangelo
    C. Motherhood
    D. Time travel

Mixed-Up Files **Study Questions**
Chapter 10

1. Who wins the game of "war" between Jamie and Mrs. Frankweiler?
   A. Jamie
   B. Mrs. Frankweiler
   C. It was a tie.
   D. It was incomplete.

2. What transportation do Claudia and Jamie take back to Greenwich?
   A. Train
   B. Police car
   C. Mrs. Frankweiler's Rolls Royce
   D. Taxi

3. What discovery does Claudia make about human nature and secrets?
   A. When you have a secret, it's no fun unless someone else knows you have one.
   B. Secrets are nothing but trouble.
   C. It isn't human nature to keep secrets; they have to be told.
   D. Secrets can be hurtful because human nature is to use secrets as bargaining power.

4. What do the children plan to do every time they save enough money?
   A. Re-visit the Metropolitan
   B. Go to New York
   C. Buy a piece of art
   D. Visit Mrs. Frankweiler

5. How do the children plan to make Mrs. Frankweiler a grandmother without her being a mother?
   A. They plan to buy her a puppy she can spoil like a grandchild.
   B. They told her she could be Angel's grandmother, since Angel was sort-of an orphan.
   C. They planned for her to marry their grandfather.
   D. They planned to secretly adopt her.

6. How is Saxonberg connected to the children?
   A. He is in charge of their trust funds.
   B. He is the museum curator who overlooked their staying at the Metropolitan.
   C. He is their grandfather.
   D. He is Mrs. Frankweiler's driver who took them home.

7. What secret does Mrs. Frankweiler keep from Claudia and Jamie?
   A. She is over a hundred years old.
   B. She and their grandfather are engaged.
   C. She once met one of Michelangelo's direct descendants in Italy.
   D. Saxonberg has been her lawyer for over 40 years.

ANSWER KEY: MULTIPLE CHOICE QUESTIONS
From the Mixed-Up Files of Mrs. Basil E. Frankweiler

	1	2	3	4	5	6	7	8	9	10
1	C	B	A	A	D	C	A	D	B	A
2	B	C	C	D	A	C	C	A	D	C
3	D	C	A	C	D	B	C	C	A	A
4	A	A	A	B	B	A		B	A	D
5	C	C	C	D	D				B	D
6	D			C	C				A	C
7	B			D					A	D
8	A			C					D	
9	D			D					B	
10									D	
11									D	
12									A	
13									C	

VOCABULARY WORKSHEETS

Mixed-Up Files **Vocabulary Worksheet**
Chapter 1
Part I: Using Prior Knowledge and Contextual Clues
Below are the sentences in which the vocabulary words appear in the text. Read the sentence. Use any clues you can find in the sentence combined with your prior knowledge, and write what you think the underlined words mean on the lines provided.

1. That last visit was the worst bore. I won't risk another dull visit for a while, so I'm having Sheldon, my <u>chauffer</u>, deliver this account to your home.

2. In the meantime she almost forgot why she was running away. But not entirely. Claudia knew that it had to do with <u>injustice</u>. She was the oldest child and the only girl and was subject to a lot of injustice.

3. She was tired of arguing about whose turn it was to choose Sunday night seven-thirty television show, of injustice, and of the <u>monotony</u> of everything.

4. Claudia also decided that she must get <u>accustomed</u> to giving up things. Learning to do without hot fudge sundaes was good practice for her.

5. She managed to shift a shallow layer of Kleenex, which her mother had used for blotting lipstick, and thus <u>exposed</u> the corner of a red ticket.

6. "I've picked you to accompany me on the greatest adventure of our <u>mutual</u> lives," Claudia repeated.

7. <u>Flattery</u> is as important a machine as the lever, isn't it, Saxonberg? Give it a proper place to rest, and it can move the world.

8. "Of course. Wearing shoes all the time is one of the <u>tyrannies</u> you'll escape by coming with me."

Mixed-Up Files **Vocabulary Worksheet**
Chapter 1 Continued

9. They <u>complemented</u> each other perfectly. She was cautious (about everything but money) and poor; he was adventurous (about everything but money) and rich.
_____

Part II: Determining the Meaning
 Match the vocabulary words to their dictionary definitions

   1. chauffeur   A. unfair treatment
   2. injustice   B. shared
   3. monotony   C. something completed something else, or made it close to perfect
   4. accustomed   D boredom that comes from doing the same thing over and over
   5. exposed   E. become used to a certain thing or way of doing things
   6. mutual   F. driver
   7. flattery   G. cruelties suffered at the hands of people in authority
   8. tyrannies   H. the act of complimenting someone for the purpose of getting something
   9. complemented I. revealed

Mixed-Up Files Vocabulary Worksheet
Chapters 2 & 3

Part I: Using Prior Knowledge and Contextual Clues

Below are the sentences in which the vocabulary words appear in the text. Read the sentence. Use any clues you can find in the sentence combined with your prior knowledge, and write what you think the underlined words mean on the lines provided.

1. A line of winter white skin was <u>punctuated</u> by his navel.

_____

2. "I'm not at <u>liberty</u> to tell. Security."

_____

3. On Wednesday come the gentle old ladies who are using the time before the Broadway <u>matinee</u> begins.

_____

4. You can tell [gentle old ladies] are a set because they wear matching pairs of <u>orthopedic</u> shoes, the kind that lace on the side.

_____

5. Jamie wished to eat in the snack bar downstairs; he thought it would be less glamorous, but cheaper, and as chancellor of the exchequer, as holder of the <u>veto</u> power, and as tightwad of the year, he got his wish.

_____

6. The bed had a tall canopy, supported by an <u>ornately</u> carved headboard at one end and by two gigantic posts at the other.

_____

7. The silence <u>seeped</u> from their heads to their soles and into their souls.

_____

Mixed-Up Files Vocabulary Worksheet
Chapters 2 & 3 Continued

Part II: Determining the Meaning
Match the vocabulary words to their dictionary definitions

1. punctuated
2. liberty
3. matinee
4. orthopedic
5. veto
6. ornately
7. seeped

A. to exercise the right to reject something
B. to end with emphasis
C. freedom to think or act
D. passed through an opening very slowly
E. an afternoon performance of a play, usually with cheaper seats than the evening performance
F. elaborately or elegantly decorated
G. relating to disorders of the bones, joints, ligaments, or muscles

Mixed-Up Files **Vocabulary Worksheet**
Chapter 4

Part I: Using Prior Knowledge and Contextual Clues
Below are the sentences in which the vocabulary words appear in the text. Read the sentence. Use any clues you can find in the sentence combined with your prior knowledge, and write what you think the underlined words mean on the lines provided.

1. Claudia hid her violin case in a sarcophagus that had no lid.

2. They went to the automat and used up a dollar's worth of Bruce's nickels. Jamie allotted ten nickels to Claudia and kept ten for himself.

3. Claudia, who had eaten cereal and drunk pineapple juice, scolded him about the need to eat properly… Jamie countered with complaints about Claudia's narrow-mindedness.

4. The pretty guide thought he was part of the class; the teacher thought that he was planted in the audience to pep up discussion; the class knew that he was an imposter.

5. The guide told Jamie that some people saved all their lives so that they could become mummies; it was indeed expensive.

6. The only real difference between [Claudia and the bronze statue of the Egyptian cat] was that the cat wore tiny golden earrings and looked a trifle less smug.

7. Mrs. Frankweiler's residence on East 63rd street was long a Manhattan showplace for what many considered one of the finest private collections of art in the Western Hemisphere. Others considered it a gigantic hodgepodge of the great and the mediocre.

Mixed-Up Files **Vocabulary Worksheet**
Chapter 4 Continued

8. Mrs. Frankweiler's residence on East 63rd street was long a Manhattan showplace for what many considered one of the finest private collections of art in the Western Hemisphere. Others considered it a gigantic hodgepodge of the great and the <u>mediocre</u>.

_____

9. Mr. Frankweiler <u>amassed</u> a fortune from the corn oil industry and from developing many corn products.

_____

10. The mystery only <u>intrigued</u> her; the magic trapped her.

_____

Part II: Determining the Meaning
Match the vocabulary words to their dictionary definitions

1. sarcophagus   A. conceited
2. allotted   B. collected over time until they form a large fund
3. countered   C. gave something to somebody as his or her share of what is available
4. imposter   D. an ancient stone or marble coffin
5. mummies   E. bodies of people that have been embalmed and wrapped in cloth, as was the custom in ancient Egypt
6. smug   F. someone who pretends to be someone he is not
7. hodgepodge   G. to say something that contradicts what someone else has said
8. mediocre   H. adequate, but not very good
9. amassed   I. to make somebody very interested
10. intrigued   J. a mixture of several unrelated things

Mixed-Up Files **Vocabulary Worksheet**
Chapter 5

Part I: Using Prior Knowledge and Contextual Clues
Below are the sentences in which the vocabulary words appear in the text. Read the sentence. Use any clues you can find in the sentence combined with your prior knowledge, and write what you think the underlined words mean on the lines provided.

1. Jamie said "NO" with such force that Claudia didn't try to persuade him.

___

2. When all was done, they were disappointed; all of it looked dismally gray.

___

3. She directed them first to the children's room, but when the librarian there found out what they wanted to know, she advised them to got to the Donnell Branch Library on Fifty-third Street.

___

4. She directed them first to the children's room, but when the librarian there found out what they wanted to know, she advised them to got to the Donnell Branch Library on Fifty-third Street.

___

5. The book also had footnotes.

___

6. Was he a juvenile delinquent? Maybe they do have his fingerprints on file.

___

7. Claudia had begun her research confident that a morning's study would make her completely an expert; but Michelangelo had humbled her, and humility was not an emotion with which she felt comfortable…

___

Mixed-Up Files **Vocabulary Worksheet**
Chapter 5 Continued

8. They bought peanuts, chestnuts, and pretzels from the <u>vendor</u> outside the museum.

_____

9. Jamie would wait twelve minutes (lag time, Claudia called it) and <u>emerge</u> from hiding.

_____

Part II: Determining the Meaning
  Match the vocabulary words to their dictionary definitions

1. persuade   A. a young person who has broken the law
2. dismally   B. someone who sells something
3. directed   C. pointed someone in a particular direction
4. advised   D. to convince or make someone believe something
5. footnotes   E. to appear
6. delinquent   F. a feeling of modesty
7. humility   G. in a depressing manner
8. vendor   H. an explanation at the bottom of a page giving further
                        information about something in the text above it
9. emerge   I. recommended

Mixed-Up Files **Vocabulary Worksheet**
Chapter 6

Part I: Using Prior Knowledge and Contextual Clues
Below are the sentences in which the vocabulary words appear in the text. Read the sentence. Use any clues you can find in the sentence combined with your prior knowledge, and write what you think the underlined words mean on the lines provided.

1. "Every morning when she got up, Mrs. Frankweiler would throw her arms about the statue, peer into its eyes, and say…

   _____

2. Footsteps from the Italian Renaissance were descending upon them!

   _____

3. They stealthily climbed the wide stairway, staying close to the rail.

   _____

4. Claudia paused to look, partly from habit and partly because anything associated with Angel was precious.

   _____

5. …Claudia and Jamie had already left and were browsing around the crowded bookshop peeking under the dust jackets of books about Michelangelo.

   _____

6. "Let's call the *New York Times*," Jamie suggested.
   "All that publicity!" They'll want to know how we found out."

   _____

Mixed-Up Files **Vocabulary Worksheet**
Chapter 6 Continued

7. "No!" Claudia screeched. "We have to know about Angel first. We have to be right."

_____

8. Knowing that everyone in that line would be shepherded in and out, in front of and past the statue in a matter of minutes, they decided to enter through the rear entrance instead.

_____

Part II: Determining the Meaning
  Match the vocabulary words to their dictionary definitions

1. peer
2. descending
3. stealthily
4. associated
5. browsing
6. publicity
7. screeched
8. shepherded

A. looking around in a leisurely manner
B. secretively or cunningly
C. guided a group of people or animals
D. made a loud, high-pitched sound
E. to look carefully, especially with narrowed eyes
F. coming down
G. public interest or knowledge
H. connected to or having to do with

Mixed-Up Files **Vocabulary Worksheet**
Chapter 7

Part I: Using Prior Knowledge and Contextual Clues
Below are the sentences in which the vocabulary words appear in the text. Read the sentence. Use any clues you can find in the sentence combined with your prior knowledge, and write what you think the underlined words mean on the lines provided.

1. Jamie scowled at Claudia. "See. I told you a stack."

_____

2. As they approached the Egyptian wing, they heard the shuffling of feet and a sound they recognized as the folding of chairs and the gathering up of rubber mats.

_____

3. Now, Saxonberg, I must tell you about that Egyptian tomb called a mastaba. It is not a whole one; it is the beginning of one.

_____

4. "Sarah looks like a pharoh. Pass it on."

_____

5. The conversation rained in softly and comfortably and told the two stowaways that they had the correct age group.

_____

6. Words continued to drizzle into their shelter.

_____

7. Claudia didn't wait to discover whether he opened it in surprise or to say something. She clamped her hand over his mouth as fast as she could.

_____

8. Why had Claudia muzzled him? Did she think he had no sense at all?

_____

Mixed-Up Files Vocabulary Worksheet
Chapter 7 Continued

Part II: Determining the Meaning
 Match the vocabulary words to their dictionary definitions

1. scowled	A. to rain lightly
2. shuffling	B. someone who hides on a traveling vessel in hopes of gaining passage without paying
3. mastaba	C. an ancient Egyptian tomb with a flat base, sloping sides, and a flat roof
4. pharaoh	D. made a facial expression characterized by drawing the eyebrows together in anger or displeasure
5. stowaway	E. to walk without picking up one's feet
6. drizzle	F. prevented a person from speaking, especially in public
7. clamped	G. a king of ancient Egypt
8. muzzled	H. held tightly over

Mixed-Up Files **Vocabulary Worksheet**
Chapter 8

Part I: Using Prior Knowledge and Contextual Clues
Below are the sentences in which the vocabulary words appear in the text. Read the sentence. Use any clues you can find in the sentence combined with your prior knowledge, and write what you think the underlined words mean on the lines provided.

1. The product of their efforts this time looked only slightly grayer than it had the time before. Claudia's sweater was considerably <u>shrunken</u>.

___

2. "The boiler on the furnace broke. No heat. They had to <u>dismiss</u> school."

___

3. Fourteen kids got cuts and <u>abrasions</u>, and their parents are suing the school to pay for their medical expenses.

___

4. The man in the derby hat was <u>scolding</u> the girl. "No wonder it takes the U.N. forever to get something done.

___

5. "How did you like those ear phones where you can tune in almost an old language at all?" Jamie asked his sister. "Pretty <u>keen</u>, huh?"

___

6. We have long known of the clue you mention; in fact, that clue remains our strongest one in <u>attributing</u> this work to the master, Michelangelo Buonarroti.

___

7. …for it is known that Michelangelo did not carve all the marble blocks which were <u>quarried</u> for him and which bore his mark.

___

8. …the work may have been done by someone else, or that someone <u>counterfeited</u> the mark into the stone much later.

___

Mixed-Up Files **Vocabulary Worksheet**
Chapter 8 Continued

9. We greatly appreciate your interest and would enjoy your <u>disclosing</u> further clues to us if you find them.

___

Part II: Determining the Meaning
Match the vocabulary words to their dictionary definitions

1. shrunken   A. areas of the skin that has been hurt by scraping
2. dismiss   B. to officially release students from school
3. abrasions   C. giving credit to a person for a particular piece of art or work of literature
4. scolding   D. obtained or gotten after much effort
5. keen   E. revealing or telling about
6. attributing   F. complaining, especially when using harsh language
7. quarried   G. slang term for "very good"
8. counterfeited   H. made a realistic copy of
9. disclosing   I. characterized by a decrease in size

Mixed-Up Files **Vocabulary Worksheet**
Chapter 9

Part I: Using Prior Knowledge and Contextual Clues
Below are the sentences in which the vocabulary words appear in the text. Read the sentence. Use any clues you can find in the sentence combined with your prior knowledge, and write what you think the underlined words mean on the lines provided.

1. "You can't call me Lady Claudia anymore. We're paupers now."
_____

2. They ascended the low, wide steps of my porch.
_____

3. I was sitting at one of the tables wearing my customary white lab coat and my baroque pearl necklace when the children were brought in.
_____

4. You must admit, Saxonberg, that when the need arises, I have a finely developed sense of theatrics.
_____

5. "We want to know about the statue," Jamie stammered.
_____

6. I summoned Parks; he appeared bearing a silver casserole.
_____

7. "You still don't think you've caused any commotion so far?"
_____

8. You must tell me all about your adventure. What you thought and what you said and how you managed to carry off the whole crazy caper."
_____

Mixed-Up Files Vocabulary Worksheet
Chapter 9 Continued

Part II: Determining the Meaning
Match the vocabulary words to their dictionary definitions

1. paupers
2. ascended
3. baroque
4. theatrics
5. stammered
6. summoned
7. commotion
8. caper

A. an ornamental style of European art (mid-16th to early 18th centuries)
B. spoke with many hesitations due to fear or strong emotion
C. a light-hearted adventure or a dangerous illegal activity
D. extremely poor individuals
E. noisy activity or confusion
F. display of false and exaggerated emotion
G. sent for someone to come
H. went upward

Mixed-Up Files Vocabulary Worksheet
Chapter 10

Part I: Using Prior Knowledge and Contextual Clues
Below are the sentences in which the vocabulary words appear in the text. Read the sentence. Use any clues you can find in the sentence combined with your prior knowledge, and write what you think the underlined words mean on the lines provided.

1. I still don't know how he does it. It was my deck of cards; but I was somewhat <u>preoccupied</u> listening to Claudia and interrupting her with questions.

   _____

2. Mrs. Kincaid kept asking if they were bruised or <u>maimed</u>.

   _____

3. "All I want are the facts and how you felt. Not a theatrical production."
   "You want me to be <u>accurate</u>, don't you?"

   _____

4. I <u>transported</u> them in the Rolls Royce as you requested.

   _____

5. He seemed to <u>regard</u> the button panel, madam, as some sort of typewriter or piano or I. B. M. computer.

   _____

6. She'll become our grandmother, then, since ours are <u>deceased</u>.

   _____

7. Suspecting that something special had <u>prompted</u> this move, I asked Sheldon to call his friend, Morris the guard, to find out if anything unusual had been discovered lately.

   _____

Mixed-Up Files Vocabulary Worksheet
Chapter 10 Continued

Part II: Determining the Meaning
Match the vocabulary words to their dictionary definitions

1. preoccupied   A. moved someone or something from one place to another, especially in a vehicle
2. maimed   B. to think of a person or thing in a particular way
3. accurate   C. totally absorbed in doing or thinking about something else
4. transported   D. affected with a severe and permanent injury
5. regard   E. precise and correct
6. deceased   F. dead
7. prompted   G. urged

VOCABULARY ANSWER KEY
From the Mixed-up Files of Mrs. Basil E. Frankweiler

	1	2&3	4	5	6	7	8	9	10
1	F	B	D	D	E	D	I	D	C
2	A	C	C	G	F	E	B	H	D
3	D	E	G	C	B	C	A	A	E
4	E	G	F	I	H	G	F	F	A
5	I	A	E	H	A	B	G	B	B
6	B	F	A	A	G	A	C	G	F
7	H	D	J	F	D	H	D	E	G
8	G		H	B	C	F	H	C	
9	C		B	E			E		
10			I						

DAILY LESSONS

Mixed-Up Files Daily Lessons

LESSON ONE

Objectives
    To introduce the novel
    To give students an overview of the unit
    To distribute books and materials relating to the unit
    To preview chapter 1

Activity #1
Bring to class several old, interesting items: an old trunk, an unusual kitchen item or farm implement or tool, a painting, an ornate glass, an old rifle, an old photo of a person or house, or an old piece of clothing, etc.

Put the items on display and give your students time to examine them. Students should not discuss anything about the items with each other. Each student should evaluate the pieces independently and silently.

After students have had time to examine the items, they should sit down at their desks and compose a story about the item of their choice. They should think about who may have owned the item, what it might have been used for, what may have happened to it in its past.

Give students ample time to complete this assignment. Ask if any students have stories they would like to share with the class. If no one does, collect the stories and read a few to the class.
This is designed more as an introductory exercise than an official writing assignment, but grade the stories if you so choose.

TRANSITION:
Explain to students that in the book they are about to read, the main characters become involved in the mystery of the history of a statue they see in The Metropolitan Museum of Art. And although the discovering the origins of the statue is important, the main character, Claudia, discovers that solving the mystery is not the only thing that will fulfill her quest.

Briefly discuss the word "quest" with your students. A synonym would be "search."

NOTE: *The idea of the Hero's Journey is one that is probably a little advanced for most students who will be reading this book; it is probably better introduced properly at a higher grade level. However, that being said, this book fits so perfectly with the idea of the Hero's Journey it would be wrong not to introduce the theme/idea on some level relating to the book.*

There are a few pages more completely describing the Hero's Journey formula following this lesson. If you have a very advanced class, you might want to share some of this information with them; however, a simple explanation or brief outline would be more practical for most classes.

Mixed-Up Files Daily Lessons

Explain to students that in its simplest form, the Hero's Journey is a kind of quest. A person leaves his/her daily routine, has experiences facing and overcoming challenges to achieve a goal, and returns a changed person.

Activity #2
Distribute the materials students will use in this unit. Explain in detail how students are to use these materials.

Study Guides Students should preview the study guide questions before each reading assignment to get a feeling for what events and ideas are important in that section. After reading the section, students will (as a class or individually) answer the question to review the important events and ideas from that section of the book. Students should keep the study guides as study materials for the unit test.

Vocabulary Prior to reading a reading assignment, students will do vocabulary work related to the section of the book they are about to read. Following the completion of the reading of the book, there will be a vocabulary review of all the words used in the vocabulary assignments. Students should keep their vocabulary work as study materials for the unit test.

Reading/Writing Assignment Sheet You need to fill in the reading assignment sheet to let students know when their reading has to be completed. You can either write the assignment sheet on a side blackboard or bulletin board and leave it there for students to see each day, or you can duplicate copies for each student to have. In either case, you should advise students to become very familiar with the reading assignments so they know what is expected of them.

Unit Outline You may find it helpful to distribute copies of the Unit Outline to your students so they can keep track of upcoming lessons and assignments. You may also want to post a copy of the Unit Outline on a bulletin board and cross off each lesson as you complete it.

Nonfiction Assignment Sheet Explain to students that they each are to read at least one non-fiction piece from the in-class library at some time during the unit. Students will fill out a nonfiction assignment sheet after completing the reading to help you evaluate their reading experiences and to help the students think about and evaluate their own reading experiences.

Extra Activities Center The Unit Resource Materials portion of this unit contains suggestions for a library of related books and articles in your classroom as well as crossword and word search puzzles. Make an extra activities center in your classroom where you will keep these materials for students to use. Bring the books and articles in from the library and keep several copies of the puzzles on hand. Explain to students that these materials are available for students to use when they finish reading assignments or other class work early.

Books Each school has its own rules and regulations regarding student use of school books. Advise students of the procedures that are normal for your school.

Mixed-Up Files Daily Lessons

Notebook or Unit Folder You may want the students to keep all of their worksheets, notes, and other papers for the unit together in a binder or notebook. During the first class meeting, tell them how you want them to arrange the folder. Make divider pages for vocabulary worksheets, study guide questions, review activities, notes, and tests. You may want to give a grade for accuracy in keeping the folder.

Activity #3
Preview the study questions for Chapter 1 with the class. (Just read through them briefly and tell students that doing this will give them clues about what is important in their upcoming reading.)

Activity #4
Do the first vocabulary worksheet for Chapter 1 orally with the class to show them how the worksheets are to be done each time. Students should write in the correct answers for study purposes.

STEPS IN THE HERO'S JOURNEY

PHASE 1: DEPARTURE

<u>The Call to Adventure</u>
The call to adventure is the point in a person's life when they are first given notice that everything is going to change, whether they know it or not.
      Questions: What stage of life is he or she in?
                         What do you see coming next for this person?
                         What would cause the person to leave this stage, "leave home"?
                         What is the person doing when the call comes? Is it an accident
                               a blunder, something planned or hoped for? Is it
                               anticipated or dreaded?

<u>Refusal of the Call</u>
Often when the call is given, the future hero refuses to heed it. This may be from a sense of duty or obligation, fear, insecurity, a sense of inadequacy, or any of a range of reasons that work to hold the person in his or her current circumstance.
      Questions: Does the hero refuse the call?
                         If so, what motivates the refusal?
                         Is the person ready to leave home, to accept adult status?
                         If not, why not?

<u>Supernatural Aid</u>
Once the hero has committed to the quest, consciously or unconsciously, his or her guide and magical helper appears, or becomes known.
      Questions: What special friends or helpers does the hero have?
                         Does the hero receive some magical help, advice, or talisman
                               from someone wise and benevolent?
                         Is there someone who helps them prepare to leave on their
                               journey?
                         Is it a one-time assistance, or will the helper(s) appear throughout
                               the journey?
                         Is the helper an internal aspect of the hero?

<u>The Crossing of the First Threshold</u>
This is the point where the person actually crosses into the field of adventure, leaving the known limits of his or her world and venturing into an unknown and dangerous realm where the rules and limits are not known.
      Questions: What world is being left; what world is being entered?
                         What or who is guarding the threshold?
                         What obstacles must the hero overcome to truly begin the journey?
                               (limits of home or society, limits of personality, limits of
                               perception, physical limits?)

Hero's Journey Page 2

The Belly of the Whale
The belly of the whale represents the final separation from the hero's known world and self. The separation has been made, or is being made. The experiences that will shape the new world and self will begin shortly, or may be beginning with this experience which is often symbolized by something, unknown, and frightening. By entering this stage the person shows their willingness to undergo a metamorphosis, to die to him or herself.

- Questions:
  - Is the person ready to transform? Does he or she enter the belly of the whale willingly, or is he/she thrust or captured in that place?
  - What self is being left? The self of childhood? Of incomplete or unfulfilled adulthood? An outgrown self?
  - What self is the person moving toward?

PHASE 2: INITIATION

The Road of Trials
The road of trials is a series of tests, tasks, or ordeals that the person must undergo to begin the transformation. Often the person fails one or more of these tests, which often occur in threes.

- Questions:
  - Given this person's background, what kinds of trials or ordeals make sense for him or her? What would be truly challenging for this person?
  - What does the person fear, and how will this fear be represented to him or her?
  - What does the person consider to be obstacles to progress or growth?
  - Does the person have some personality or character traits that will be mirrored back to him/her in a challenging way?
  - What strategies, skills, insights, known or unknown strengths or talents, etc., does the person use or develop to survive or resolve these trials?
  - What assistance, seen or unseen, does the person have or receive to deal with these trials?

The Meeting With the Goddess
This represents the point in the adventure when the person experiences a love that has the power and significance of the all-powerful, all encompassing, unconditional love that a fortunate infant may experience with his or her mother. It may be represented by the person finding the other person that he or she loves most completely.

- Questions:
  - How is this step be represented in the story?
  - Does the person have a soul mate, an other half?
  - Does the person begin to understand or experience the union of opposites, for example spiritual/material, good/bad, male/female, life/death, etc.?

Hero's Journey Page 3

Woman as Temptress
This step is about those temptations that may lead the hero to abandon or stray from his or her quest. Woman is a metaphor for physical or material temptations of life, since the hero-knight was often tempted from his spiritual journey by lust.

> Questions: Given this person's background and experience, what kinds of temptations make sense for him or her?
> Is this person on a spiritual journey; will he/she experience temptations of the flesh?
> Are there habitual patterns of thought or behavior that serve to undermine or tempt the person from his/her path?

Atonement With the Father
In this step the person must confront and be initiated by whatever holds the ultimate power in his or her life. In many myths and stories, this is the father or a father figure who has life and death power. It is the center point of the journey. All the previous steps have been moving toward this place; all that follow will move out from it. For the transformation to take place, the person as he or she has been must be "killed" so that the new self can come into being. Sometimes this killing is literal; sometimes it is metaphorical.

> Questions: How does the person resolve him/herself with the sources of control and power in his/her life?
> What experiences mark the person as ready to take on the new roles of his/her transformed self?
> What behaviors, attitudes, relationships, dependencies, body parts must be sacrificed to achieve this?

Apotheosis
To apotheosize is to deify. When someone dies a physical death, or dies to the self to live in spirit, he or she moves beyond the pairs of opposites to a state of divine knowledge, love, compassion, and bliss. This is a god-like state; the person is in heaven and beyond all strife.

> Questions: What would heaven be for this person?
> What does this person know or experience now that is beyond good and evil, male and female, life and death?
> Does the person give him/herself a moment to bask in the glow of what has been achieved?

The Ultimate Boon
This is the achievement of the goal of the quest. It is what the person went on the journey to get. All the previous steps serve to prepare and purify the person for his step, since in many myths the boon is something transcendent like the elixir of life itself, or a plant that supplies immortality, or the holy grail.

> Questions: What would be the goal of this person's quest? What is the ultimate boon for this person?
> Was there a stated goal of the quest? If so has it changed? Has the person learned more or less than he/she expected?

Hero's Journey Page 4

What are the rewards of the person's journey?
What relationship does this person now have to his/her own mortality, gods, or god-like figures?

PART 3: RETURN

Refusal of the Return
So when all has been achieved, why come back to normal life?
- Questions: Does the person refuse to come back to everyday life?
  Is the person concerned that their message won't be heard, or that their gifts will be unappreciated, or that the wisdom gained can not be communicated?

The Magic Flight
Sometimes the hero must escape with the boon, if it is something that the gods have been jealously guarding. It can be just as adventurous and dangerous returning from the journey as it was to go on it.
- Questions: Are there obstacles to the person's returning to normal life?
  Will these obstacles further enlighten us about the person, their quest, or their boon?

Rescue from Without
Just as the hero may need guides and assistants to set out on the quest, oftentimes he or she must have powerful guides and rescuers to bring them back to everyday life, especially if the person has been wounded or weakened by the experience. Or perhaps the person doesn't realize that it is time to return, that they can return, or that others need their boon.
- Questions: Must the person be rescued from their journey?
  Can their original guides and assistants still help them?

Crossing the Return Threshold
The trick in returning is to retain the wisdom gained on the quest, to integrate that wisdom into a human life, and then maybe figure out how to share the wisdom with the rest of the world. This is usually extremely difficult.
- Questions: What marks the person's return to normal life?
  What challenges does the person face in integrating the experience of the quest into his or her life?
  Can/does the person share his or her experiences and the wisdom gained from them with others?
  How do others receive the person upon the return?

Hero's Journey Page 5

Master of Two Worlds

For a human hero, this may mean achieving a balance between the material and spiritual. The person has become comfortable and competent in both the inner and outer worlds.

    Questions: What would represent the two worlds in his/her life?

    Does this person demonstrate his/her mastery of the spiritual and material, the inner and outer, the two worlds?

Freedom to Live

Mastery leads to freedom from the fear of death, which in turn is the freedom to live. This is sometimes referred to as living in the moment, neither anticipating the future nor regretting the past.

    Question: Does the person achieve the ability to let go of the fear of death, to live in the moment, to neither anticipate the future nor regret the past?

Mixed-Up Files Daily Lessons

LESSON TWO

Objectives
    To read Chapter 1
    To evaluate students' oral reading
    To introduce the KWL Worksheet and Characterization Chart
    To preview the study questions for Chapter 2
    To complete the vocabulary worksheet for Chapters 2 & 3

Activity #1
Have students read Chapter 1 of *From the Mixed-Up Files* aloud. You probably know the best way to select readers in your classroom: pick students at random, ask for volunteers, or use whatever method works best for your group. If you have not yet completed an oral reading evaluation for your students this marking term, this would be a good opportunity to do so. A form is included for your convenience.

Activity #2
Take a few minutes to do a simple thinking exercise with your students. Rather than charging on to the study questions or the next reading assignment, take a few minutes to do a KWL exercise. If you're not familiar with KWL, it's very simple, and a worksheet follows. Basically, fill in one column stating what you (the students) **K**now so far based on their reading of Chapter 1. In the middle column, write down what you (the students) **W**ant to know–questions that are unanswered in the first chapter. As students continue to read the book, they can jot down things they **L**earn as they read. This is a short, little thing you can do to encourage students to think about their reading. Pull it out once and a while at the end of every chapter or every few chapters to see what more has been added in the L column.

Activity #3
As you read *From the Mixed-Up Files of Mrs. Basil E. Frankweiler*, students should keep an individual character chart for either Claudia or Jamie. Students should list the character's name, as well as words and phrases that describe that character's appearance, personality, or actions–along with the page numbers on which they find the quotes. A sample chart can be found on the next page. You might ask half the class to make a character map for Jamie while the other half completes a map for Claudia.

Distribute the sample chart to each student and fill in a line or two for each character as a class to give students the idea as to how to do it.

Activity #4
Students should use the remaining class time to preview the study questions and do the vocabulary worksheet for Chapters 2 & 3. This assignment should be completed prior to the next class period.

KWL
From the Mixed-Up Files of Mrs. Basil E. Frankweiler

Directions: Before reading, think about what you already know about *From the Mixed-Up Files of Mrs. Basil E. Frankweiler*. Write the information in the **K** column. Think about what you would like to find out from reading the book. Write your questions in the **W** column. After you have read the book, use the **L** column to write the answers to your questions from the W column, and anything else you remember from the book.

K **What I Know**	**W** **What I Want to Find Out**	**L** **What I Learned**

CHARACTERIZATION CHART
From the Mixed-Up Files of Mrs. Basil E. Frankweiler

Use the table below to organize details about a character's appearance, personality, or actions. You may decide to write a quote from the novel–in which case you should be sure to use quotation marks and note the page on which the quote appears, or you may paraphrase the information (put it into your own words)–in which case you would NOT need quotation marks.

Character's Name _____

Appearance	Personality	Actions	Page Number

ORAL READING EVALUATION
From the Mixed-Up Files of Mrs. Basil E. Frankweiler

Name _____ Class _____ Date _____

SKILL	EXCELLENT	GOOD	AVERAGE	FAIR	POOR
FLUENCY	5	4	3	2	1
CLARITY	5	4	3	2	1
AUDIBILITY	5	4	3	2	1
PRONUNCIATION	5	4	3	2	1
_____	5	4	3	2	1
_____	5	4	3	2	1

TOTAL GRADE _____

COMMENTS:

Mixed-Up Files Daily Lessons

LESSON THREE

Objectives
    To review the main events and ideas from Chapter 1
    To check the vocabulary worksheets for Chapters 2 & 3
    To read Chapter 2
    To evaluate students' oral reading

Activity #1
Give students a few minutes to formulate answers for the study questions for Chapter 1 and then discuss the answers to the questions in detail. Write the answers on the board or overhead transparency so students can have the correct answers for study purposes.

NOTE: It is a good practice in public speaking and leadership skills for individual students to take charge of leading the discussions of the study questions. Perhaps a different student could go to the front of the class and lead the discussion each day that the study questions are discussed in this unit. Of course, you should guide the discussion when appropriate and try to fill in any gaps students may leave. The study questions could really be handled in a number of different ways, including in small groups with group reports following. Occasionally you may want to use the multiple choice questions as quizzes to check students' reading comprehension. As a short review now and then, students could pair up for the first (or last, if you have time left at the end of a class period) few minutes of class to quiz each other from the study questions. Mix up methods of reviewing the materials and checking comprehension throughout the unit so students don't get bored just answering the questions the same way each day. Variety in methods will also help address the different learning styles of your students. From now on in this unit, the directions will simply say, "Discuss the answers to the study questions in detail as previously directed." You will choose the method of preparation and discussion each day based on what best suits you and your class.

Activity #2
Take a few minutes to discuss the correct answers to the vocabulary worksheet for Chapters 2 & 3 so students have the correct answers for study purposes. You might want to post the answers to the vocabulary matching section on one section of your board and add each chapter's answers on the day that students should have completed them. If students get in the habit of checking them first thing when they come in (maybe while you take attendance), it will save you the time of going through the answers during the class period. You may occasionally wish to spot-check students' vocabulary work prior to posting the answers–just to make sure they're doing it and not just copying the answers.

Activity #3
Read Chapter 2. If you have not completed the oral reading evaluations, continue with those until all students have been evaluated. When all students have been evaluated, students may read silently, in pairs or small groups, or orally as a class. Reading instructions for the remainder of the unit will simply say, Read Chapter __." You will choose how your students read (silently, orally, in pairs or groups, etc.) based on what best suits you and your class. Usually a variety of reading strategies is best to give students the opportunity to comprehend the information from a variety of ways.

Activity #4
Students should preview the study questions for Chapter 3 prior to the next class meeting.

Mixed-Up Files Daily Lessons

LESSON FOUR

Objectives
> To review the main events and ideas from Chapter 2
> To introduce students to the non-fiction reading assignment
> To give students time to work on the non-fiction assignment
> To read Chapter 3

Activity #1
Discuss the study questions for Chapter 2 in detail, as previously directed.

Activity #2
Distribute copies of the Non-fiction Reading Assignment. Explain to students that they are expected to read some non-fiction work related to *From the Mixed-Up Files of Mrs. Basil E. Frankweiler* and complete this worksheet regarding their reading. Some suggested topics are listed below. You could assign one of these topics to each student, let students pick their own topics from this list, or let students choose a topic of their own as long as it is related to the novel. Later in the unit students will give brief oral reports about their reading. This will make students recall their reading, give them an opportunity to practice public speaking, and expose all students to a variety of non-fiction information about topics related to the book.

Take students to the place in your school where they can find non-fiction information and give them ample time to find resource materials on their topics. Students should find information, read about their topics, and complete the non-fiction assignment sheet.

Topic Suggestions (all mentioned in the novel):

Daniel Boone	Henry Hudson	Joan of Arc
Marie Antoinette	Italian Renaissance	Clara Barton
Michelangelo	Leonardo Di Vinci	Florence Nightingale
Sistine Chapel	David and Moses	Pagan
Mona Lisa	Rockefeller Center	Angel
Mastaba	United Nations	Saving money
Sir Lawrence Olivier	Metropolitan Museum of Art	Cost of transportation
Mah-jong	Farmington, CT	5th Avenue, NY City
Transistor radio	Woolworth's	42nd Street, NY City
Neanderthal Man	Madison Avenue, New York	

Activity #3
If students finish the non-fiction assignment prior to the end of the class time, they should read Chapter 3. This reading assignment should be completed by all students prior to the next class meeting.

NONFICTION ASSIGNMENT SHEET
From the Mixed-Up Files of Mrs. Basil E. Frankweiler
(To be completed after reading the required nonfiction article.)

Name _____ Date _____ Class _____

Title of Nonfiction Read _____

Written by _____ Publication Date _____

Web Site Address (if applicable) _____

I. Factual Summary: Write a summary of the piece you read.

II. Vocabulary:
    1. Which vocabulary words were difficult?

    2. What did you do to help yourself understand the words?

III. Interpretation: What was the main point the author wanted you to get from reading his/her work?

IV. Criticism:
    1. Which points of the piece did you agree with or find easy to believe? Why?

    2. With which points of the piece did you disagree or find difficult to believe? Why?

V. Personal Response:
    1. What did you think about this piece?

    2. How does this piece help you understand the novel better?

Mixed-Up Files Daily Lessons

LESSON FIVE

Objectives
        To review the main ideas and events from Chapter 3
        To update students' character charts and KWL worksheets
        To explore the idea of "secrets"
        To preview the study questions and do the vocabulary worksheet for Chapter 4
        To read Chapter 4

Activity #1
Discuss the answers to the study questions for Chapter 3 in detail, as previously directed.

Activity #2
Give students 5-10 minutes to update their character charts and KWL worksheets.

Activity #3
Pose the following questions regarding "secrets" to your students. Write their responses on the board or use them as a springboard for a class discussion. The idea here is to get students to think about secrets–kinds of secrets, things that are best kept as secrets and things that shouldn't be kept as secrets. Secrets, by their very nature, often require us to make moral and ethical decisions. Discuss these ideas with your students.

What is a secret?
Are there different kinds of secrets?
Should you promise to keep secrets all the time? Or only if you feel you can keep the secret?
Are there some secrets that should not be kept?
        How about a woman who has breast cancer? Should she tell her family?
        How about a pregnant teen?
        How about if you know someone who uses illegal drugs?
        How about if you know a crime has been committed?
How important is it to keep a secret if someone talks to you in confidence?
What are some "harmless" secrets to keep?
Are there times when keeping secrets from someone can hurt them–either by the nature of the secret
        or simply by hurting their feelings by being excluded?
Is a secret as in a *mysterious* secret different from a *personal* secret?
Why was Angel's secret important to Claudia?

Activity #4
In the remaining class time, students should preview the study questions, do the vocabulary worksheet, and read Chapter 4. This assignment should be completed prior to the next class meeting.

Mixed-Up Files Daily Lessons

LESSON SIX

Objectives
    To review the main ideas and events of Chapter 4
    To preview an issue of *The New York Times*
    To write a personal response
    To evaluate students' writing
    To preview the study questions and do the vocabulary worksheet for Chapter 5
    To read Chapter 5

Activity #1
Discuss the answers to the study questions for Chapter 4 in detail, as previously directed.

Activity #2
Acquire enough issues of a *New York Times* for each student to have one. They all don't have to be exactly the same; they can be from different days. Give each student a paper. Ask how many students have read a *New York Times* before. Tell a little about the newspaper–that it's read world-wide, etc. Show students the parts of the newspaper. Have students orally read a few headlines from each section. In the story, Claudia and Jamie acquire a *New York Times* newspaper to find out about the statue. Ask students in what section that kind of information might be available. Give students about 15 minutes to read an article or two of their choice from the paper.

[If you have Internet access, take your students on-line to the web site of the *New York Times* (www.nytimes.com). Compare and contrast the electronic newspaper/website to the printed newspaper.]

Activity #2
Distribute Writing Assignment #1. Discuss the directions in detail, and give students ample time to complete the assignment.

Activity #3
When students finish the writing assignment, they should preview the study questions, do the vocabulary worksheet for Chapter 5, and read Chapter 5. This assignment should be completed prior to the next class meeting.

WRITING ASSIGNMENT #1
From the Mixed-Up Files of Mrs. Basil E. Frankweiler
Expressing Personal Responses In Writing

PROMPT
Claudia and Jamie looked in the *New York Times* for information about the statue. Scan the newspaper you have been given for headlines that look interesting to you. After you have scanned through the whole paper, go back and read 2 or 3 short articles or 1-2 long articles of your choice. After you have read them, choose one article, write a report and response for it, citing the newspaper article as your source.

PREWRITING
Think about the articles you have read. Which one was the most interesting to you? Why? What are the topics of the articles? Do any of the articles stir up your opinions or emotions? Why? What do you think about the topics being discussed? Which article would you have the most to say in response? Write about that article.

DRAFTING
At the top of your page, use your usual heading for this class. Then, cite the newspaper. Follow this format:
   SOURCE:
   Author. "Title or Headline of The Article." Name of the Newspaper Date of the newspaper dd Month Year: SectionPage.

An example would be:
   SOURCE:
   Di Rado, Alicia. "Trekking through College." Los Angeles Times 15 March 1995: A3.

Skip two lines and write the heading "REPORT." Write a paragraph summarizing the article.

An example would be:
   REPORT
   The article cited above is about college students who belong to a Star Trek fan club. They meet weekly to watch the television show together, and once a month they have a "swap meet" where they exchange memorabilia. Once a year they go together to a Star Trek convention.

Skip two lines and write the heading "RESPONSE." Write a paragraph or two clearly stating your response to the article. Did you agree or disagree with it? What did you think of it. What are your personal opinions? Use a topic sentence and then explain it.

Mixed-Up Files Writing Assignment #1, page 2

An example would be:
>RESPONSE
>
>I think being a part of a Star Trek fan club is a great idea for college students. It would be a good way to relax after classes or on the weekends and to be with friends who have the same interest. Watching one television show together weekly wouldn't cut into studying time very much, and trading stuff on the weekends could be a lot of fun. As long as the fan club wouldn't interfere with getting good grades, it seems like good thing to do. Although I personally don't like Star Trek and wouldn't want to be in that fan club, I could see that some people would really enjoy it.
>
>If I were at college, I think I'd rather spend my spare time playing basketball than being in a fan club. Basketball is something I've always liked to do. Like the fan club, it would give me a way to relax, have fun, and get together with my friends. It's good that there are a lot of things to choose from to do in our spare time!

PROMPT
When you finish the rough draft, ask a student who sits near you to read it. After reading your rough draft, he/she should tell you what he/she liked best about your work which parts were difficult to understand, and ways in which your work could be improved. Re-read your paper considering your critic's comments. Make the corrections you think are necessary.

PROOFREADING
Do a final proofreading of your paper, double-checking your grammar, spelling, organizations, and the clarity of your ideas.

Mixed-Up Files Daily Lessons

LESSONS SEVEN AND EIGHT

Objectives
> To review the main events and ideas from Chapter 5
> To preview the study questions and do the vocabulary worksheets for Chapters 6-8
> To read Chapters 6-8

Activity #1
Discuss the answers to the study questions for Chapter 5 in detail, as previously directed.

Activity #2
NOTE: *Essentially, students will be completing the same work for Chapters 6-8 as they did for the previous five chapters; however, they will be reading and studying Chapters 6-8 in a literature circle format in order to mimic the teamwork Claudia and Jamie share in the novel.*

Divide students into pairs. Explain to them that over the next two days they will be responsible for previewing and answering the study guide questions for Chapters 6-8, completing the vocabulary worksheets for chapters 6-8, reading Chapters 6-8. Each group will determine how to accomplish these tasks–what each group member's responsibility will be, which work will be complete in class, and how reading assignments will be completed. All of the work must be completed by Lesson Nine (give students a day/date).

Advise students that there will be a test on Chapters 6-8 in Lesson Nine to check their work. Tell them if they have any questions at all, they should talk to you as you circulate around the room.

Circulate through the classroom and talk with individual groups over the next two days to maintain order and clarify any points of confusion the students may have about the novel. This is also a good opportunity for you to discuss the novel with smaller groups of students and gauge reactions to the text.

NOTE: *If your students work well independently, this would be a good time to hold individual writing conferences if you have completed grading Writing Assignment #1. Actually, Writing Assignment #1 is so short, you could grade the paper with the student sitting next to you, making comments, explanations, and suggestions as you grade it. A Writing Evaluation Form is included with this unit for your convenience.*

WRITING EVALUATION FORM
From The Mixed-Up Files of Mrs. Basil E. Frankweiler

Writing Assignment # ___

Name _____ Date _____

Grade ___

Circle One For Each Item:

Grammar:	correct	errors noted on paper
Spelling:	correct	errors noted on paper
Punctuation:	correct	errors noted on paper
Legibility:	excellent	good fair poor
_____	excellent	good fair poor
_____	excellent	good fair poor

Strengths:

Weaknesses:

Comments/Suggestions:

Mixed-Up Files Daily Lessons

LESSON NINE

Objectives
> To review the main events and ideas from Chapters 6-8
> To check students' work from Lessons Seven and Eight

Activity #1
Distribute the Chapter 6-8 Quizzes. Give students ample time to complete them. Have students swap papers for grading. Give students the correct answers so they can grade the papers. Collect the papers for viewing and/or recording the grades.

NOTE: The quizzes have the same questions as the study guides. Be sure to return the quizzes to students so they can have them for studying.

Activity #2
Discuss the answers to the multiple choice sections of the vocabulary worksheets for Chapter 6, Chapter 7, and Chapter 8.

Activity #3
Take a few minutes to discuss the idea of "heroism" that was introduced in Chapter 8. Claudia says:

> "I feel as if I jumped into a lake to rescue a boy, and what I thought was a boy turned out to be a wet, fat log. Some heroine that makes. All wet for nothing."

Discuss these questions:

What had Claudia received that turned her "boy" into a "wet, fat log"?
What makes a hero? What things are necessary for one to be called a "hero"?
Who are some classic heroes?
Who are some of your heroes?
Once a person is a hero, are they always a hero? Can you be un-hero-ed?
Do you think Claudia will be a "hero" by the end of the book? (Come back to this question again after students have read the entire book.)

Activity #4
If time remains, students can update their KWL worksheets and their character charts.

QUIZ CHAPTERS 6-8
From the Mixed-Up Files of Mrs. Basil E. Frankweiler

1. What does Claudia notice about the velvet that rested underneath Angel?
    A. It looks just like her curtains at home.
    B. It is not really velvet.
    C. It is marked by an impression from the bottom of the statue.
    D. It is her favorite color.

2. What conclusion do Claudia and Jamie draw after looking at the velvet?
    A. It was originally commissioned for an Olympic event.
    B. It was stolen.
    C. It was created by Michelangelo.
    D. It was created by someone whose name began with "W."

3. What do the siblings decide to do about their new knowledge?
    A. Write an article for the newspaper explaining their findings.
    B. Write a letter to the museum explaining their findings.
    C. Write a letter to their parents explaining their findings.
    D. Save the information for some later time when it would be more useful.

4. Why won't Claudia return home without discovering who created "Angel"?
    A. She won't be any "different" if they don't find out about Angel.
    B. The whole reason for leaving home was to find out about Angel; she doesn't want to go until her mission is accomplished.
    C. If they solve the riddle, their leaving home and breaking the rules might be forgiven.
    D. She wants to collect the reward money for solving the mystery.

5. How do Claudia and Jamie justify spending so much of their money on a mailbox rental?
    A. They can replace the funds.
    B. They are going home the next day.
    C. They are expecting a large sum of money to be sent to the mailbox.
    D. They use money from the wallet they found.

6. Who do the siblings run into in the mastaba?
    A. Their mother
    B. The security guards
    C. Jamie's classmates
    D. A janitor

7. How does Claudia use the encounter in the mastaba to her advantage?
    A. She finds a good place to hide.
    B. She overhears two knowledgeable museum patrons talking about Angel.
    C. She is able to have Jamie deliver a letter to the museum officials without giving away his identity.
    D. She gets some of Jamie's friends to sneak them some food.

Mixed-Up Files Quiz Chapters 6-8 Continued

8. Where do the children decide to spend the majority of their day on Tuesday?
    A. Researching Angel
    B. Resting
    C. Studying in the museum
    D. Touring the U.N.

9. Why does Claudia cry when she reads the letter from the museum officials?
    A. The letter of rejection is so polite that she can't be angry; just sad.
    B. The letter tells how worried her parents are.
    C. The letter tells that Angel is being moved to a different museum.
    D. The letter says the mystery has already been solved.

10. Why isn't Claudia ready to go home yet?
    A. She hasn't heard from her parents.
    B. She hasn't seen enough of the city on her own.
    C. She hasn't accomplished anything.
    D. She hasn't gotten over being angry.

11. To where does Claudia want to buy tickets?
    A. Italy
    B. Farmington, CT
    C. Home
    D. New York

MATCHING:

____ 12. Scowled   A. Prevents a person from speaking, especially in public

____ 13. Pharaoh   B. Giving credit to a person for a particular piece of artwork

____ 14. Muzzles   C. Connected to or having to do with

____ 15. Abrasions   D. Coming down

____ 16. Attributing   E. A king of ancient Egypt

____ 17. Disclosing   F. Revealing or telling about

____ 18. Descending   G. Looking around in a leisurely manner

____ 19. Associated   H. Areas of skin that have been hurt by scraping

____ 20. Browsing   I. Made a facial expression characterized by drawing the eyebrows together in anger or displeasure

ANSWER KEY: QUIZ CHAPTERS 6-8
From the Mixed-Up Files of Mrs. Basil E. Frankweiler

1. C
2. C
3. B
4. A
5. A
6. C
7. C
8. D
9. A
10. C
11. B
12. I
13. E
14. A
15. H
16. B
17. F
18. D
19. C
20. G

Mixed-Up Files Daily Lessons

LESSON TEN

Objectives
    To focus on Claudia's trait of planning and bring it into real life
    To practice writing to inform
    To evaluate students' writing
    To preview the study questions and vocabulary for Chapter 9
    To read Chapter 9

Activity #1
Distribute Writing Assignment #2 and discuss the directions in detail. Give students ample time to complete the assignment. Tell students when the assignments are due.

Activity #2
Students should preview the study questions and do the vocabulary worksheet for Chapter 9, then they should read Chapter 9. Students may begin this assignment if they finish the writing assignment prior to the end of the class time. All students should complete this assignment prior to the next class meeting.

LESSON ELEVEN

Objectives
    To review the main events and ideas from Chapter 9
    To preview the study questions and do the vocabulary worksheet for Chapter 10
    To read Chapter 10

Activity #1
Discuss the answers to the study questions for Chapter 9 in detail, as previously directed. Take an extra few minutes to preview the questions for Chapter 10.

Activity #2
Do the vocabulary worksheet for Chapter 10 orally together as a class.

Activity #3
Have students read Chapter 10, either orally or silently–whichever best suits.

WRITING ASSIGNMENT #2
From the Mixed-Up Files of Mrs. Basil E. Frankweiler
Writing To Inform

PROMPT
You have seen time and time again that Claudia is a *planner*. It's what she does; she plans for every detail she can imagine. Having a goal and a plan is important, but you also need to be prepared to change your plans if something goes awry or if an opportunity presents itself. Claudia was intrigued by Angel, saw an opportunity, and adjusted her plans accordingly.

What are your plans? Do you have any? Are you planning your education? A vacation? Do you daydream about future wedding plans? Career plans? Family plans? Strategy for winning a sports game or improving your skills at a sport or hobby? Perhaps you'd like to renovate your bedroom. Your assignment is to write a letter informing Claudia of your plans and asking if she has any advice for you (since she seems to be a planning expert!).

PREWRITING
Make a list of things you are planning. If you are not planning *anything*, you'll need to take an extra step and think of something to plan. Write down your plans in as much detail as possible. Do things need to be done in a specific order? Do you need to acquire materials, information, or help to carry out your plans? Make lists of anything you might need and jot down notes about how and where you will get it.

DRAFTING
This will be an informal letter, so put the date at the top, left-hand, first line of your paper. Skip a line and write, "Dear Claudia," (or if you know her really well, you could call her Claude like Jamie does!). Introduce your plans and let Claudia know you're hoping she will consider your plans and write back with any suggestions or advice. In the next paragraphs, as needed, lay out your plans in detail so Claudia can see exactly what you have in mind. Tell her every detail you know so that she can give you back helpful advice. Be sure to use a closing paragraph thanking her for taking the time to read your plan and again politely asking for her advice. Be sure to tell her how to get in contact with you to reply. Make an informal closing (such as "Your fan" or "Your friend," or "Sincerely.") and sign your name (legibly!).

PROMPT
When you finish the rough draft, ask a student who sits near you to read it. After reading your rough draft, he/she should tell you what he/she liked best about your work which parts were difficult to understand, and ways in which your work could be improved. Re-read your paper considering your critic's comments. Make the corrections you think are necessary.

PROOFREADING
Do a final proofreading of your paper, double-checking your grammar, spelling, organizations, and the clarity of your ideas.

Mixed-Up Files Daily Lessons

LESSON TWELVE

Objectives
    To review the main events and ideas from Chapter 10
    To return to the idea of the Hero's Journey
    To share information from the non-fiction assignment
    To practice public speaking

Activity #1
Discuss the answers to the study questions for Chapter 10 as previously directed.

Activity #2
Return to the idea of the Hero's Journey with your class for a few minutes. Based on the depth in which you explained the idea in Lesson One, discuss Claudia's character throughout the book with regard to this theme. Here are a few brief points which might be helpful in your discussion:

    The Call to Adventure: Claudia is mad at her parents and thinks about running away from home.
    The Refusal of the Call: Claudia decides she doesn't really want to run away; rather, she decides to run TO something, to have an adventure.
    Supernatural Aid: Although Jamie isn't supernatural, she does choose him to help her on her quest since he would be a good companion, has money sense and money.
    Crossing the First Threshold: Claudia and Jamie leave the bus and get on the train, re-emerging in Grand Central Station in New York.
    Belly of the Whale: Claudia and Jamie enter the museum
    Road of Trials: Getting situated at the museum, avoiding being detected, figuring out how to live at the museum
    Meeting With the Goddess: Angel is introduced. Claudia thinks Angel looks like her.
    Woman as Temptress: The letter tempted Jamie to quit. He could see no further reason to continue the adventure. Claudia was tempted to quit, but she had to keep searching for the thing that would make her return "different."
    Atonement With the Father: Claudia and Jamie meet Mrs. Frankweiler, the person with the information Claudia needs to complete her quest
    Ultimate Boon: Claudia finds the file and the sketch; the mystery of Angel is solved.
    Refusal of the Return: Claudia still doesn't want the adventure to be over.
    Magic Flight: Claudia's obstacles to returning to "normal" life are rooted in her desire to go home "different." She must negotiate with Mrs. Frankweiler to achieve her desired goal before she returns home.
    Rescue from Without: Mrs. Frankweiler acts as the catalyst to help Claudia return home by filling Claudia's need and literally sending her home in the Rolls.
    Crossing the Return Threshold: Claudia learned that having a secret is only fun if someone knows you have one. Claudia finally understands what she wanted.
    Master of two Worlds: Claudia and Jamie return home and vow to "adopt" Mrs. Frankweiler, visiting her as often as they can. They can move easily between the two worlds.

NOTE: *You don't need to use all of this stuff; it is here if you think your students will benefit from it, but it isn't essential to understanding the book. Use your discretion as to how much of the analysis you pursue with your class.*

Mixed-Up Files Daily Lessons

LESSONS THIRTEEN AND FOURTEEN

Objective
    To discuss the book on a deeper than direct-recall level, exploring the themes
    and many ideas presented in the book

Activity
The pages which follow contain critical thinking and personal response questions as well as quotations from the novel. Choose the questions/quotes which would be most appropriate for the level of your students.

There are many different ways to use these questions and quotations. You could assign one question to each student in your class, give students time to prepare responses, and then use the students' oral responses as jumping-off points for discussions. You could divide your class into pairs or small groups and assign each pair or small group a question to answer and then have the groups give short oral presentations. Each group could be responsible for leading a discussion about one question and one quotation. You could have all students formulate answers for all the questions and then discuss them as a class. As always, you're free to think of other creative ways to use the questions! Whatever way you choose, we have allotted two class periods to the end of discussing many aspects of the novel and its themes.

LESSON FIFTEEN

Objectives
    To give students the opportunity to practice writing persuasively
    To evaluate students' writing
    To review the events and characters in the novel

Activity
Distribute Writing Assignment #3, discuss the directions in detail, and give students ample time to complete the assignment. Tell students when their compositions are due.

CRITICAL THINKING/DISCUSSION QUESTIONS
From the Mixed-up Files of Mrs. Basil E. Frankweiler

Interpretation

1. Who is the narrator? How does she influence the plot in the novel?

2. What are the main conflicts in the novel, and how are they resolved (if they are)? Consider both internal and external conflicts.

3. List the main characters in the novel and list three characteristics (two positive and one negative) of each one.

4. What is the point of view throughout the novel? Does it change? Why is the point-of-view important in this book?

5. What is the setting of this novel? Why is the setting important?

6. What elements in the story make it realistic?

7. Where is the high point of the action (the climax) in the story?

Critical

8. How does Claudia's relationship with Jamie change throughout the novel? What events bring about these changes?

9. What roles do the parents and grandparents play in the novel? Compare and contrast the adults in the novel and tell how they influence the younger characters.

10. Why is Angel important in the novel? What does it symbolize?

11. In what ways are Claudia and Jamie a "family of two?"

12. Compare and contrast Claudia and Mrs. Frankweiler.

13. Compare and contrast Jamie and Mrs. Frankweiler.

14. Compare and contrast Claudia and Jamie.

15. What is Saxonberg's purpose in the novel? What would the novel lack without his character?

16. What indications do we have that Saxonberg, Mrs. Frankweiler, Claudia, Jamie, and Angel are connected, even before Claudia realizes it herself?

17. What is the importance of planning in the book? Are do all plans go smoothly? If not, what changes have to be made to whose plans?

18. Humor is important in the book. Describe 5 humorous incidents in the book.

Mixed-Up Files Critical Thinking/Discussion Questions Continued

19. What things create the element of suspense in the book?

20. Why is it ironic that the expression Jamie often uses is, "Baloney!"

21. What did the detail about Mrs. Frankweiler's wanting to experience motherhood add to the story?

22. Why does Claudia run away? For what is she searching? Does she find it?

23. Explain the title of the novel, *From the Mixed-up Files of Mrs. Basil E. Frankweiler.*

24. In what ways are Claudia and Jamie typical siblings? In what ways are they extraordinary?

Critical/Personal Response
25. Who is your favorite character? Why? Find a passage from the novel that contains a description of your character or that demonstrates the quality that you most admire.

Personal Response
26. Have you ever been fascinated by a place, person, activity, or topic? Describe.

27. With whom (from the novel) would you most like to be friends?

28. With whom do you most identify? Why?

29. What is your favorite scene, moment, or line from the novel? Why?

QUOTATIONS
From the Mixed-Up Files of Mrs. Basil E. Frankweiler

1. "In the meantime she almost forgot why she was running away. But not entirely. Claudia knew that it had to do with injustice. She was the oldest child and the only girl and was subject to a lot of injustice" (6).

2. "Claudia loved the city because it was elegant; it was important; and busy. The best place in the world to hide" (8).

3. "Besides, once she made up her mind to go, she enjoyed the planning almost as much as she enjoyed spending money. Planning long and well was one of her special talents." (9)

4. "Kevin never realized then or ever that he had been given a clue, and he pouted all the way home" (18).

5. "For the first time, the meaning instead of the grammar of what Claudia had said penetrated" (24).

6. "'One was a note to Mom and Dad to tell them that we are leaving home and not to call the FBI. They'll get it tomorrow or the day after'"(26).

7. "It's not my money we're spending. It's *our* money. We're in this together, remember?" (28).

8. "Claudia would never have permitted herself to become so overheated, but Jamie liked perspiration, a little bit of dirt, and complications." (33)

9. "What happened was: they became a team, a family of two. There had been times before they ran away when they had acted like a team, but those were very different from feeling like a team' (39).

10. "Five-thirty in winter is dark, but nowhere seems as dark as the Metropolitan Museum of Art. The ceilings are so high that they fill up with a lot of darkness" (40).

11. "Next to any kind of elegance, Claudia loved good, clean smells" (44).

12. "If you think of doing something in New York City, you can be certain that at least two thousand other people have that same thought. And of the two thousand who do, about one thousand will be standing in line waiting to do it." (50)

13. "Claudia had found the article about the statue too easily. She didn't even look at the first section of the paper. I keep telling you that often the search proves more profitable than the goal. Keep that in mind when you're looking for something in my files" (61).

14. "…Michelangelo? I truly believe that this name has magic even now; the best kind of magic because it comes from true greatness. Claudia sensed it as she again stood in the line. The mystery only intrigued her; the magic trapped her." (65).

Mixed-Up Files Quotations Continued

15. "She would solve its mystery; and it, in turn, would do something important to her, though what this was, she didn't quite know" (65).

16. "Both Jamie and Claudia had acquired a talent for being near but never part of a group. (Some people, Saxonberg, never learn to do that all their lives, and some learn it all too well.) (66)

17. "Yeah, I guess homesickness is like sucking your thumb. It's what happens when you're not very sure of yourself." (86)

18. "You know, Claude, when I'm not wishing I could give you a sock right in the nose, I'm glad you're on my team. You're smart even if you're hard to live with." (108)

19. "But we never even used your radio. How can we face them at home? Without the radio and all. With nothing." (117)

20. "Well, Claude, we just traded safety for adventure. Come along, Lady Claudia." (125)

21. "'You see,' I laughed, 'under the fancy trappings, I'm just a plain lady.'" (137)

22. "Claudia said, "But, Mrs. Frankweiler, you should want to learn one new thing every day. We did even at the museum."

    "No," I answered, " I don't agree with that. I think you should learn, of course, and some days you must learn a great deal. But you should also have days when you allow what is already in you to swell up inside of you until it touches everything. And you can feel it inside you. If you never take time out to let that happen, then you must accumulate facts, and they begin to rattle around inside of you. You can make noise with them, but never really feel anything with them. It's hollow."

23. "'I need having the secret more than I need the money,' I told him. I knew that Claudia understood. Jamie looked puzzled." (148)

WRITING ASSIGNMENT #3
From the Mixed-Up Files of Mrs. Basil E. Frankweiler
Writing To Persuade

PROMPT
Can you imagine being Claudia and Jamie and having to return home after being gone on such an adventure for so many days? Would your parents/guardians be upset with you if you would do such a thing? Most parents would probably be *very* upset! They would be relieved to know you are safe and glad to have you home again, but they would likely be pretty angry with you, too, for leaving.

Your assignment is to write a letter from Mrs. Frankweiler to Mr. and Mrs. Kincaid persuading them not to be too harsh on Claudia and Jamie upon their return.

PREWRITING
Why shouldn't Claudia and Jamie be grounded for life for pulling such a stunt? Think of as many reasons as you can, and jot them down on a piece of paper. When possible jot down examples to support your claims. Then, go back and look at your notes. Which reasons are the best, the most persuasive? Concentrate mostly on them as you put together your letter. Remember, you are not recounting the events of the story; you are persuading Mr. and Mrs. Kincaid to take it easy on the kids.

DRAFTING
If you have time, create letterhead stationery for Mrs. Frankweiler. Date your letter and begin with the salutation, "Dear Mr. and Mrs. Kincaid,". In the first paragraph introduce yourself. (Remember you are Mrs. Frankweiler.) Explain the purpose of your letter. In the body paragraphs of the letter, give your reasons why the Kincaids should be lenient on the children. Use one paragraph for each main reason. Within the paragraph use examples or explanations to support and clarify your point. Write a closing paragraph in which you express your interest in the children and make some nice closing remarks. Use an appropriate closing, like "Sincerely yours," or "With best wishes," or something similar. Sign your name (legibly).

PROMPT
When you finish the rough draft, ask a student who sits near you to read it. After reading your rough draft, he/she should tell you what he/she liked best about your work which parts were difficult to understand, and ways in which your work could be improved. Re-read your paper considering your critic's comments. Make the corrections you think are necessary.

PROOFREADING
Do a final proofreading of your paper, double-checking your grammar, spelling, organizations, and the clarity of your ideas.

Mixed-Up Files Daily Lessons

LESSON SIXTEEN

Objective
    To review the vocabulary words studied in this unit

Activity
Choose one or more of the vocabulary review activities listed and spend your class time as directed in the activity.

LESSON SEVENTEEN

Objective
    To review the events and ideas presented in this unit

Activity #1
Take a few minutes to review the character charts and the KWL worksheets students have been keeping throughout the unit.

Activity #2
Choose one or more of the unit review activities listed and spend your class time as directed in the activity.

VOCABULARY REVIEW ACTIVITIES
From the Mixed-Up Files of Mrs. Basil E. Frankweiler

Divide your class into two teams and have an old-fashioned spelling or definition bee.

Give each of your students (or students in groups of two, three or four) a *From the Mixed-up Files of Mrs. Basil E. Frankweiler* Vocabulary Word Search Puzzle. The person (group) to find all of the vocabulary words in the puzzle first wins.

Give students a *From the Mixed-up Files of Mrs. Basil E. Frankweiler* Vocabulary Word Search Puzzle without the word list. The person or group to find the most vocabulary words in the puzzle wins.

Use a *From the Mixed-up Files of Mrs. Basil E. Frankweiler* Vocabulary Crossword Puzzle. Put the puzzle onto a transparency on the overhead projector (so everyone can see it), and do the puzzle together as a class.

Give students a *From the Mixed-up Files of Mrs. Basil E. Frankweiler* Vocabulary Matching Worksheet to do.

Divide your class into two teams. Use *From the Mixed-up Files of Mrs. Basil E. Frankweiler* vocabulary words with their letters jumbled as a word list. Student 1 from Team A faces off against Student 1 from Team B. You write the first jumbled word on the board. The first student (1A or 1B) to unscramble the word wins the chance for his/her team to score points. If 1A wins the jumble, go to student 2A and give him/her a definition. He/she must give you the correct spelling of the vocabulary word that fits that definition. If he/she does, Team A scores a point, and you give student 3A a definition for which you expect a correctly spelled matching vocabulary word. Continue giving Team A definitions until some team member makes an incorrect response. An incorrect response sends the game back to the jumbled-word face off, this time with students 2A and 2B. Instead of repeatedly giving definitions to the first few students of each team, continue with the student after the one who gave the last incorrect response on the team. For example, if Team B wins the jumbled-word face-off, and student 5B gave the last incorrect answer for Team B, you would start this round of definition questions with student 6B, and so on. The team with the most points wins!

Have students write a story in which they correctly use as many vocabulary words as possible. Have students read their compositions orally! Post the most original compositions on your bulletin board!

UNIT REVIEW GAMES/ACTIVITIES
From the Mixed-up Files of Mrs. Basil E. Frankweiler

Ask the class to make up a unit test for *From the Mixed-up Files of Mrs. Basil E. Frankweiler.* The test should have 4 sections: matching, true/false, short answer, and essay. Students may use 1/2 period to make the test and then swap papers and use the other 1/2 class period to take a test a classmate has devised. (open book). You may want to use the unit test included in this packet or take questions from the students' unit tests to formulate your own test.

Take 1/2 period for students to make up true and false questions (including the answers). Collect the papers and divide the class into two teams. Draw a big tic-tac-toe grid on the chalkboard. Make one team X and one team O. Ask questions to each side, giving each student one turn. If the question is answered correctly, that student's team's letter (X or O) is placed in the box. If the answer is incorrect, no letter is placed in the box. The object is to get three in a row like tic-tac-toe. You may want to keep track of the number of games won for each team.

Take 1/2 period for students to make up questions (true/false and short answer). Collect the questions. Divide the class into two teams. Alternate asking questions to individual members of teams A & B (like in a spelling bee). The question keeps going from A to B until it is correctly answered, then a new question is asked. A correct answer does not allow the team to get another question. Correct answers are +2 points; incorrect answers are -1 point.

Have students pair up and quiz each other from their study guides and class notes.

Give students a *From the Mixed-up Files of Mrs. Basil E. Frankweiler* crossword puzzle to complete.

Divide your class into two teams. Use *From the Mixed-up Files of Mrs. Basil E. Frankweiler* crossword words with their letters jumbled as a word list. Student 1 from Team A faces off against Student 1 from Team B. You write the first jumbled word on the board. The first student (1A or 1B) to unscramble the word wins the chance for his/her team to score points. If 1A wins the jumble, go to student 2A and give him/her a clue. He/she must give you the correct word which matches that clue. If he/she does, Team A scores a point, and you give student 3A a clue for which you expect another correct response. Continue giving Team A clues until some team member makes an incorrect response. An incorrect response sends the game back to the jumbled-word face off, this time with students 2A and 2B. Instead of repeating giving clues to the first few students of each team, continue with the student after the one who gave the last incorrect response on the team. For example, if Team B wins the jumbled-word face-off, and student 5B gave the last incorrect answer for Team B, you would start this round of clue questions with student 6B, and so on. The team with the most points wins!

Play "What's My Line?" This is similar to the old television show. Students assume the roles of different characters from the novel. One student gives clues to the class or a panel of contestants. The contestants try to guess the identity of the guest. Students may enjoy assisting you in creating rules and procedures for the game.

Mixed-Up Files Unit Review Activities Continued

Play Jeopardy. Divide the class into two groups. Assign each group a category or book from the epic and have them devise answers for that category. Play the game according to the television show procedures.

Play "Drawing in the Details." This is similar to "Pictionary." Divide students into teams. A student from one team draws a scene from the novel. Drawings should be kept simple, to keep the pace lively. Students on the opposing team locate the scene in their books and read it aloud. If they are incorrect, the illustrator's team has a chance to guess. Involve students in setting up a scoring system and any other necessary rules.

UNIT TESTS

SHORT ANSWER UNIT TEST 1
From the Mixed-Up Files of Mrs. Basil E. Frankweiler

I. Matching/Identify

___ 1. ADOPT   A. Short for The Metropolitan Museum of Art

___ 2. JAMIE   B. Mrs. Frankweiler's butler

___ 3. MUSEUM   C. How Claudia and Jamie travel to Farmington, Connecticut

___ 4. KONIGSBURG   D. Playing cards and the fountain are sources of this.

___ 5. SECRET   E. Strolling down _____ Avenue may cause Claudia to shop.

___ 6. MET   F. Place Claudia and Jamie go to research Michelangelo

___ 7. TAXI   G. Sold Angel to the Metropolitan Museum of Art

___ 8. FARMINGTON   H. Impossible thing Mrs. Frankweiler would like to be

___ 9. COINS   I. He created Angel.

___10. MONEY   J. Claudia uses her ____ case as a suitcase.

___11. FIFTH   K. Claudia and Jamie skip school by hiding in the school ____.

___12. VIOLIN   L. Author of From The Mixed Up Files of Mrs. Basil E. Frankweiler

___13. MOTHER   M. Being away from home is not making Claudia and Jamie ____.

___14. LIBRARY   N. Place Claudia hides her violin case

___15. CLAUDIA   O. Number of hours the kids have to find the secret.

___16. PARKS   P. Claudia and Mrs. Frankweiler both like keeping these.

___17. SARCOPHAGUS   Q. Jamie is carrying $24.43 worth of these in his pockets.

___18. VELVET   R. Place Claudia and Jamie run away to

___19. ONE   S. Town where Mrs. Frankweiler lives

___20. BUS   T. He makes extra money gambling at cards.

___21. BRUCE   U. Angel left three rings with an

___22. HOMESICK   V. She plans to run away.

___23. MICHELANGELO   W. He plays cards with Jamie on the school bus.

___24. DIFFERENT   X. The children plan to secretly _____ Mrs. Frankweiler.

___25. FRANKWEILER   Y. Claudia wanted to return home this way.

Mixed-Up Files Short Answer Unit Test 1 Page 2

II. Short Answer

1. What is one of Claudia's special talents? Give 2 examples.

2. Who are the recipients of the letters Claudia mails on the day they leave home?

3. What is Claudia's plan for closing time at the museum on the first day?

4. How do the children choose to spend their days at the museum?

5. Why do the siblings go to 42nd Street? How do they get there?

6. Where do Claudia and Jamie find unexpected income?

7. What does Claudia notice about the velvet that rested underneath Angel?

8. Why won't Claudia return home without discovering who created "Angel"?

Mixed-Up Files Short Answer Unit Test 1 Page 3

9. Why does Claudia cry when she reads the letter from the museum officials?

10. Who does Mrs. Frankweiler call while the children are waiting to see her?

11. Why doesn't Claudia want to tell Mrs. Frankweiler where she and Jamie stayed all week?

12. What are the terms of Mrs. Frankweiler's bargain regarding finding the secret of Angel?

13. What deal does Mrs. Frankweiler make with Jamie and Claudia?

14. What discovery does Claudia make about human nature and secrets?

15. How is Saxonberg connected to the characters in the novel?

Mixed-Up Files Short Answer Unit Test 1 Page 4

III. Composition

1. List three characteristics (two positive and one negative) of Claudia, Jamie, and Mrs. Frankweiler.

   Claudia:

   Jamie:

   Mrs. Frankweiler

2. Why is Angel important in the novel? What does "she" symbolize?

3. Compare and contrast Claudia and Mrs. Frankweiler.

Mixed-Up Files Short Answer Unit Test 1 Page 5

4. Humor is important in the book. Describe 2 humorous incidents in the book.

5. What things create the elements of suspense in the book?

6. Why does Claudia run away? For what is she searching? Does she find it?

Mixed-Up Files Short Answer Unit Test 1 Page 6

IV. Quotations: Choose 3 of the following quotes and explain the significance of each. Identify the quotes you use by the number.

1. "Claudia had found the article about the statue too easily. She didn't even look at the first section of the paper. I keep telling you that often the search proves more profitable than the goal. Keep that in mind when you're looking for something in my files" (61).

2. "…Michelangelo? I truly believe that this name has magic even now; the best kind of magic because it comes from true greatness. Claudia sensed it as she again stood in the line. The mystery only intrigued her; the magic trapped her." (65).

3. "She would solve its mystery; and it, in turn, would do something important to her, though what this was, she didn't quite know" (65).

4. "Claudia said, "But, Mrs. Frankweiler, you should want to learn one new thing every day. We did even at the museum."

5. "'I need having the secret more than I need the money,' I told him. I knew that Claudia understood. Jamie looked puzzled." (148)

Mixed-Up Files Short Answer Unit Test 1 Page 7

V. Vocabulary

Write the vocabulary words you are given. After writing them down, go back and write in their definitions.

Word	Definition
1	
2	
3	
4	
5	
6	
7	
8	
9	
10	

SHORT ANSWER UNIT TEST 1 ANSWER KEY
From the Mixed-Up Files of Mrs. Basil E. Frankweiler

I. Matching/Identifying

X	1. ADOPT	A.	Short for The Metropolitan Museum of Art
T	2. JAMIE	B.	Mrs. Frankweiler's butler
R	3. MUSEUM	C.	How Claudia and Jamie travel to Farmington, Connecticut
L	4. KONIGSBURG	D.	Playing cards and the fountain are sources of this.
P	5. SECRET	E.	Strolling down _____ Avenue may cause Claudia to shop.
A	6. MET	F.	Place Claudia and Jamie go to research Michelangelo
C	7. TAXI	G.	Sold Angel to the Metropolitan Museum of Art
S	8. FARMINGTON	H.	Impossible thing Mrs. Frankweiler would like to be
Q	9. COINS	I.	He created Angel.
D	10. MONEY	J.	Claudia uses her ____ case as a suitcase.
E	11. FIFTH	K.	Claudia and Jamie skip school by hiding in the school ____.
J	12. VIOLIN	L.	Author of From The Mixed Up Files of Mrs. Basil E. Frankweiler
H	13. MOTHER	M.	Being away from home is not making Claudia and Jamie ____.
F	14. LIBRARY	N.	Place Claudia hides her violin case
V	15. CLAUDIA	O.	Number of hours the kids have to find the secret.
B	16. PARKS	P.	Claudia and Mrs. Frankweiler both like keeping these.
N	17. SARCOPHAGUS	Q.	Jamie is carrying $24.43 worth of these in his pockets.
U	18. VELVET	R.	Place Claudia and Jamie run away to
O	19. ONE	S.	Town where Mrs. Frankweiler lives
K	20. BUS	T.	He makes extra money gambling at cards.
W	21. BRUCE	U.	Angel left three rings with an
M	22. HOMESICK	V.	She plans to run away.
I	23. MICHELANGELO	W.	He plays cards with Jamie on the school bus.
Y	24. DIFFERENT	X.	The children plan to secretly _____ Mrs. Frankweiler.
G	25. FRANKWEILER	Y.	Claudia wanted to return home this way.

Mixed-Up Files Short Answer Unit Test 1 Answer Key Page 2

II. Short Answer

1. What is one of Claudia's special talents? Give 2 examples.
    Claudia could plan long and well. ADD TO ANSWER

2. Who are the recipients of the letters Claudia mails on the day they leave home?
    One envelope contains a letter to their parents, explaining that they have run away. The other envelope is going to the corn flakes company for a 25 cent box top rebate.

3. What is Claudia's plan for closing time at the museum on the first day?
    The siblings will go to the restrooms right before closing time and hide in the stalls–"feet up, head down, door open."

4. How do the children choose to spend their days at the museum?
    Claudia decides that they should learn everything they can about the museum.

5. Why do the siblings go to 42nd Street? How do they get there?
    They walk to the library on 42nd Street in order to conduct research about Michelangelo and the Renaissance.

6. Where do Claudia and Jamie find unexpected income?
    They find coins in the fountain where they bathe.

7. What does Claudia notice about the velvet that rested underneath Angel?
    An impression was made by the statue and memorized by the velvet–three rings with an "M" (the children suppose) in the middle of one of the rings.

8. Why won't Claudia return home without discovering who created "Angel"?
    She believes that making this discovery would allow her to go home "different."

9. Why does Claudia cry when she reads the letter from the museum officials?
    She doesn't know what else to do about a "polite letter of rejection." She feels they have accomplished nothing because they did not accomplish their goal of solving the mystery surrounding "Angel."

10. Who does Mrs. Frankweiler call while the children are waiting to see her?
    She calls Saxonberg.

11. Why doesn't Claudia want to tell Mrs. Frankweiler where she and Jamie stayed all week?
    She wants to have a secret, just as Mrs. Frankweiler holds the secret about "Angel."

Mixed-Up Files Short Answer Unit Test 1 Answer Key Page 3

12. What are the terms of Mrs. Frankweiler's bargain regarding finding the secret of Angel?
    Mrs. Frankweiler gives the pair one hour to find the secret about Angel in her filing cabinets. At the end of the hour, the pair will give her the details of their week at the Met, and Frankweiler will have her driver, Sheldon, take them home.

13. What deal does Mrs. Frankweiler make with Jamie and Claudia?
    If they promise not to tell the secret of Angel while Mrs. Frankweiler is alive, she will bequeath the sketch to them in her will.

14. What discovery does Claudia make about human nature and secrets?
    ". . . after a time having a secret and nobody knowing you have a secret is no fun. And although you don't want others to know what the secret is, you want them to at least know you have one."

15. How is Saxonberg connected to the characters in the novel?
    He is Mrs. Frankweiler's attorney and Claudia's and Jamie's grandfather.

III & IV. Compositions and Quotations: You need to grade these answers according to your own expectations of your students and your class discussions.

V. Vocabulary Use this space to write the words and definitions you wish to use for the tests.

Word	Definition
1	
2	
3	
4	
5	
6	
7	
8	
9	
10	

SHORT ANSWER UNIT TEST 2
From the Mixed-Up Files of Mrs. Basil E. Frankweiler

I. Matching/Identify

___ 1. HOMESICK   A. Claudia's special talent

___ 2. KONIGSBURG   B. The children plan to secretly _____ Mrs. Frankweiler.

___ 3. PLANNING   C. Place Claudia and Jamie go to research Michelangelo

___ 4. STATUE   D. Number of hours the kids have to find the secret.

___ 5. CLAUDIA   E. Claudia sends for a rebate from this type of company.

___ 6. PILLOW   F. Jamie suggests fingerprinting this for clues.

___ 7. FOUNTAIN   G. Jamie flatters Claudia by calling her ____.

___ 8. ATTORNEY   H. He plays cards with Jamie on the school bus.

___ 9. SAXONBERG   I. Place Claudia and Jamie bathe

___ 10. BRUCE   J. Jamie is carrying $24.43 worth of these in his pockets.

___ 11. SHELDON   K. Short for The Metropolitan Museum of Art

___ 12. ADOPT   L. Sold Angel to the Metropolitan Museum of Art

___ 13. COINS   M. He makes extra money gambling at cards.

___ 14. SKETCH   N. Occupation of Claudia and Jamie's grandfather.

___ 15. FRANKWEILER   O. Claudia and Jamie take a tour of the ____.

___ 16. SARCOPHAGUS   P. Mrs. Frankweiler's driver

___ 17. LIBRARY   Q. She plans to run away.

___ 18. JAMIE   R. Mrs. Frankweiler's butler

___ 19. BRILLIANT   S. Author of From The Mixed Up Files of Mrs. Basil E. Frankweiler

___ 20. MET   T. Mrs. Frankweiler plans to bequeath this to the children.

___ 21. MOTHER   U. Claudia places Jamie's instructions for running away here.

___ 22. PARKS   V. Being away from home is not making Claudia and Jamie ____.

___ 23. U. N.   W. Impossible thing Mrs. Frankweiler would like to be

___ 24. ONE   X. Place Claudia hides her violin case

___ 25. CEREAL   Y. Mrs. Frankweiler's lawyer

Mixed-Up Files Short Answer Unit Test 2 Page 2

II. Short Answer

1. How does Jamie make extra money?

2. Why does Claudia suggest they skip Fifth Avenue?

3. What do Claudia and Jamie do until 5:30 PM on their first day at the museum?

4. How does Claudia plan to focus their learning at the museum after discovering Angel?

5. How do Claudia and Jamie divide their research project?

6. Describe Claudia's and Jamie's discussion about homesickness.

7. What conclusion do Claudia and Jamie draw after looking at the velvet?

8. How does Claudia us the encounter in the mastaba to her advantage?

Mixed-Up Files Short Answer Unit Test 2 Page 3

9. Why isn't Claudia ready to go home after receiving the letter from the museum officials?

10. How do the children spend the last of their money?

11. What secret does Jamie share with Mrs. Frankweiler?

12. What do Claudia and Jamie find in the file labeled "Bologna, Italy"?

13. What is the one "impossible" thing that Mrs. Frankweiler would like to experience?

14. What do the children plan to do every time they save enough money?

15. What secret does Mrs. Frankweiler keep from Claudia Jamie?

Mixed-Up Files Short Answer Unit Test 2 Page 4

III. Composition

1. Who is the narrator? How does she influence the plot in the novel?

2. Where is the high point of the action (the climax) in the story?

3. In what ways are Claudia and Jamie a "family of two?"

Mixed-Up Files Short Answer Unit Test 2 Page 5

4. Compare and contrast Claudia and Jamie.

5. Humor is important in the book. Describe 2 humorous incidents in the book.

6. Why is it ironic that the expression Jamie often uses is, "Baloney!"

7. Explain the tile of the novel, *From the Mixed-up Files of Mrs. Basil E. Frankweiler.*

Mixed-Up Files Short Answer Unit Test 2 Page 6

IV. Quotations: Choose 3 of the following quotes and explain the significance of each. Identify the quotes you use by the number.

1. "Claudia had found the article about the statue too easily. She didn't even look at the first section of the paper. I keep telling you that often the search proves more profitable than the goal. Keep that in mind when you're looking for something in my files" (61).

2. "...Michelangelo? I truly believe that this name has magic even now; the best kind of magic because it comes from true greatness. Claudia sensed it as she again stood in the line. The mystery only intrigued her; the magic trapped her." (65).

3. "She would solve its mystery; and it, in turn, would do something important to her, though what this was, she didn't quite know" (65).

4. "Claudia said, "But, Mrs. Frankweiler, you should want to learn one new thing every day. We did even at the museum."

5. "'I need having the secret more than I need the money,' I told him. I knew that Claudia understood. Jamie looked puzzled." (148)

From the Mixed-Up Files Short Answer Unit Test 2 Page 7

V. Vocabulary
   Write the vocabulary words you are given. After writing them down, go back and write in their definitions.

Word	Definition
1	
2	
3	
4	
5	
6	
7	
8	
9	
10	

ANSWER KEY: SHORT ANSWER UNIT TEST 2
From the Mixed-Up Files of Mrs. Basil E. Frankweiler

I. Matching/Idendifying

V	1. HOMESICK	A. Claudia's special talent
S	2. KONIGSBURG	B. The children plan to secretly _____ Mrs. Frankweiler.
A	3. PLANNING	C. Place Claudia and Jamie go to research Michelangelo
F	4. STATUE	D. Number of hours the kids have to find the secret.
Q	5. CLAUDIA	E. Claudia sends for a rebate from this type of company.
U	6. PILLOW	F. Jamie suggests fingerprinting this for clues.
I	7. FOUNTAIN	G. Jamie flatters Claudia by calling her _____.
N	8. ATTORNEY	H. He plays cards with Jamie on the school bus.
Y	9. SAXONBERG	I. Place Claudia and Jamie bathe
H	10. BRUCE	J. Jamie is carrying $24.43 worth of these in his pockets.
P	11. SHELDON	K. Short for The Metropolitan Museum of Art
B	12. ADOPT	L. Sold Angel to the Metropolitan Museum of Art
J	13. COINS	M. He makes extra money gambling at cards.
T	14. SKETCH	N. Occupation of Claudia and Jamie's grandfather.
L	15. FRANKWEILER	O. Claudia and Jamie take a tour of the _____.
X	16. SARCOPHAGUS	P. Mrs. Frankweiler's driver
C	17. LIBRARY	Q. She plans to run away.
M	18. JAMIE	R. Mrs. Frankweiler's butler
G	19. BRILLIANT	S. Author of From The Mixed Up Files of Mrs. Basil E. Frankweiler
K	20. MET	T. Mrs. Frankweiler plans to bequeath this to the children.
W	21. MOTHER	U. Claudia places Jamie's instructions for running away here.
R	22. PARKS	V. Being away from home is not making Claudia and Jamie ___.
O	23. U. N.	W. Impossible thing Mrs. Frankweiler would like to be
D	24. ONE	X. Place Claudia hides her violin case
E	25. CEREAL	Y. Mrs. Frankweiler's lawyer

Mixed-Up Files Short Answer Unit Test 2 Anser Key Page 2

II. Short Answer

1. How does Jamie make extra money?
    He makes extra money by gambling at cards, playing "war" with Bruce.

2. Why does Claudia suggest they skip Fifth Avenue?
    She sarcastically hints that strolling down 5th Avenue might make her want to shop.

3. What do Claudia and Jamie do until 5:30 PM on their first day at the museum?
    They wander around the museum looking for a place to spend the night.

4. How does Claudia plan to focus their learning at the museum after discovering Angel?
    She decides to focus their learning on Michelangelo and determining whether or not he actually created "Angel." She decides they will continue to learn something about everything else in the museum, as well, though not to the same extent she had initially planned.

5. How do Claudia and Jamie divide their research project?
    Claudia assigns Jamie the task of looking through books for pictures of "Angel," while she concentrates on reading.

6. Describe Claudia's and Jamie's discussion about homesickness.
    Claudia and Jamie attempt to discover why they are not homesick. They recall the time when they had to stay with their aunt while their mother had a baby and that they were homesick then. They come to the conclusion that they are more sure of themselves and better trained, which is why they are not homesick this time.

7. What conclusion do Claudia and Jamie draw after looking at the velvet?
    They decide to investigate the mark further since Jamie can recall seeing the mark on one of the books during the previous day's research. They discover that the mark is Michelangelo's stonemason's mark.

8. How does Claudia use the encounter in the mastaba to her advantage?
    She is going to have Jamie deliver the letter and claim to be from the third-grade class visiting from Greenwich. He can further claim to be Bruce Lansing–"but only if they ask."

9. Why isn't Claudia ready to go home after receiving the letter from the museum officials?
    She can't explain it, but she feels that a "real discovery will help" her return home as a changed individual.

10. How do the children spend the last of their money?
    They purchase taxi fare to Farmington from Hartford, Connecticut.

Mixed-Up Files Short Answer Unit Test 2 Anser Key Page 3

11. What secret does Jamie share with Mrs. Frankweiler?
    He tells her that he and Claudia have been staying at the Metropolitan all week.

12. What do Claudia and Jamie find in the file labeled "Bologna, Italy"?
    They find a two-sided document. On side one is written a sonnet by Michelangelo. Side two contains a sketch of Angel.

13. What is the one "impossible" thing that Mrs. Frankweiler would like to experience?
    She would like to be a mother.

14. What do the children plan to do every time they save enough money?
    They plan to visit Mrs. Frankweiler.

15. What secret does Mrs. Frankweiler keep from Claudia and Jamie?
    Their grandfather has been her lawyer for forty-one years.

III & IV. Compositions and Quotations: You need to grade these answers according to your own expectations of your students and your class discussions.

V. Vocabulary Use this space to write the words and definitions you wish to use for the tests.

Word	Definition
1	
2	
3	
4	
5	
6	
7	
8	
9	
10	

ADVANCED SHORT ANSWER UNIT TEST
From the Mixed-Up Files Of Mrs. Basil E. Frankweiler

I. Matching/Identifying

___ 1. HOMESICK   A. Claudia's special talent
___ 2. KONIGSBURG   B. The children plan to secretly _____ Mrs. Frankweiler.
___ 3. PLANNING   C. Place Claudia and Jamie go to research Michelangelo
___ 4. STATUE   D. Number of hours the kids have to find the secret.
___ 5. CLAUDIA   E. Claudia sends for a rebate from this type of company.
___ 6. PILLOW   F. Jamie suggests fingerprinting this for clues.
___ 7. FOUNTAIN   G. Jamie flatters Claudia by calling her ____.
___ 8. ATTORNEY   H. He plays cards with Jamie on the school bus.
___ 9. SAXONBERG   I. Place Claudia and Jamie bathe
___ 10. BRUCE   J. Jamie is carrying $24.43 worth of these in his pockets.
___ 11. SHELDON   K. Short for The Metropolitan Museum of Art
___ 12. ADOPT   L. Sold Angel to the Metropolitan Museum of Art
___ 13. COINS   M. He makes extra money gambling at cards.
___ 14. SKETCH   N. Occupation of Claudia and Jamie's grandfather.
___ 15. FRANKWEILER   O. Claudia and Jamie take a tour of the ____.
___ 16. SARCOPHAGUS   P. Mrs. Frankweiler's driver
___ 17. LIBRARY   Q. She plans to run away.
___ 18. JAMIE   R. Mrs. Frankweiler's butler
___ 19. BRILLIANT   S. Author of From The Mixed Up Files of Mrs. Basil E. Frankweiler
___ 20. MET   T. Mrs. Frankweiler plans to bequeath this to the children.
___ 21. MOTHER   U. Claudia places Jamie's instructions for running away here.
___ 22. PARKS   V. Being away from home is not making Claudia and Jamie ____.
___ 23. U. N.   W. Impossible thing Mrs. Frankweiler would like to be
___ 24. ONE   X. Place Claudia hides her violin case
___ 25. CEREAL   Y. Mrs. Frankweiler's lawyer

Mixed-Up Files Advanced Short Answer Unit Test Page 2

II. Short Answer

1. List three characteristics (two positive and one negative) of Claudia, Jamie, and Mrs. Frankweiler.

   Claudia:

   Jamie:

   Mrs. Frankweiler:

2. Why is Angel important in the novel? What does "she" symbolize?

3. In what ways are Claudia and Jamie a "family of two?"

Mixed-Up Files Advanced Short Answer Unit Test Page 3

4. Compare and contrast Jamie and Mrs. Frankweiler.

5. Compare and contrast Claudia and Jamie.

6. Humor is important in the book. Describe 5 humorous incidents in the book.

Mixed-Up Files Advanced Short Answer Unit Test Page 4

7. Why does Claudia run away? For what is she searching? Does she find it?

8. Explain the title of the novel, *From the Mixed-up Files of Mrs. Basil E. Frankweiler.*

Mixed-Up Files Advanced Short Answer Unit Test Page 5

III. Essay

Answer one of the following questions in a complete essay form.

1. Explain how the Hero's Journey theme applies to *From The Mixed-Up Files of Mrs. Basil E. Frankwiler*.

2. Defend this quote from the School Library Journal's review of *From The Mixed-Up Files of Mrs. Basil E. Frankwiler*:
   > "All [readers] hope for in a book: humor, suspense, intrigue, and their problems acknowledge seriously but not somberly."

Mixed-Up Files Advanced Short Answer Unit Test Page 6

V. Vocabulary
    Write down the vocabulary words given, then write a paragraph or two about *From the Mixed-Up Files of Mrs. Basil E. Frankweiler* correctly using 10 of the words.

MULTIPLE CHOICE UNIT TEST 1
From the Mixed-Up Files of Mrs. Basil E. Frankweiler

I. Matching

___ 1. ANGEL   A. The statue with a secret.
___ 2. ATTORNEY   B. Author of From The Mixed Up Files of Mrs. Basil E. Frankweiler
___ 3. CLAUDIA   C. Short for The Metropolitan Museum of Art
___ 4. MONEY   D. Angel left three rings with an
___ 5. LIBRARY   E. Mrs. Frankweiler's lawyer
___ 6. MICHELANGELO   F. Jamie flatters Claudia by calling her ____.
___ 7. PLANNING   G. Mrs. Frankweiler asks Parks to bring her one.
___ 8. FRANKWEILER   H. Place Claudia and Jamie go to research Michelangelo
___ 9. SECRET   I. The children are driven home in a ____ Royce.
___10. TAXI   J. Occupation of Claudia and Jamie's grandfather.
___11. DIFFERENT   K. She plans to run away.
___12. STATUE   L. He created Angel.
___13. CEREAL   M. How Claudia and Jamie travel to Farmington, Connecticut
___14. PARKS   N. Playing cards and the fountain are sources of this.
___15. SAXONBERG   O. Being away from home is not making Claudia and Jamie ___.
___16. JAMIE   P. Strolling down _____ Avenue may cause Claudia to shop.
___17. BRILLIANT   Q. Sold Angel to the Metropolitan Museum of Art
___18. HOMESICK   R. Claudia's special talent
___19. MET   S. Claudia and Mrs. Frankweiler both like keeping these.
___20. MIRROR   T. He makes extra money gambling at cards.
___21. SONNET   U. Claudia wanted to return home this way.
___22. FIFTH   V. Jamie suggests fingerprinting this for clues.
___23. KONIGSBURG   W. Claudia sends for a rebate from this type of company.
___24. VELVET   X. Mrs. Frankweiler's butler
___25. ROLLS   Y. One was written on the back of a sketch of Angel.

Mixed-Up Files Multiple Choice Unit Test 1 Page 2

II. Multiple Choice

1. What is one of Claudia's special talents?
    A. Dancing
    B. Playing the violin
    C. Planning
    D. Singing

2. Who are the recipients of the letters Claudia mails on the day they leave home?
    A. The President and the FBI
    B. Claudia's and Jamie's best friends
    C. Her parents and a cereal company
    D. Her parents and The Metropolitan Museum

3. What is Claudia's plan for closing time at the museum on the first day?
    A. Leave through the front door and re-enter through the back
    B. Call their parents to come get them
    C. Leave with one of the families in the museum
    D. Climb into the sarcophagus

4. How do the children choose to spend their days at the museum?
    A. They plan to sit in the snack bar and watch people go by.
    B. They plan to learn as much as they can about one gallery per day.
    C. They plan to create a map of the museum so they can find their way around.
    D. They plan to draw pictures of their favorite rooms in the museum.

5. Why do the siblings go to 42nd Street?
    A. To conduct research at the library
    B. To shop
    C. To eat lunch
    D. To visit Mrs. Frankweiler

6. Where do Claudia and Jamie find unexpected income?
    A. Tip money left for waitresses in the snack bar
    B. Change left behind at the vending machines
    C. A lost wallet in the restroom
    D. Coins in their bathing fountain

7. What does Claudia notice about the velvet that rested underneath Angel?
    A. It looks just like her curtains at home.
    B. It is not really velvet.
    C. It is marked by an impression from the bottom of the statue.
    D. It is her favorite color.

Mixed-Up Files Multiple Choice Unit Test 1 Page 3

8. Why won't Claudia return home without discovering who created "Angel"?
    A. She won't be any "different" if they don't find out about Angel.
    B. The whole reason for leaving home was to find out about Angel; she doesn't want to go until her mission is accomplished.
    C. If they solve the riddle, their leaving home and breaking the museum rules might be forgiven.
    D. She wants to collect the reward money for solving the mystery.

9. Why does Claudia cry when she reads the letter from the museum officials?
    A. The letter of rejection is so polite that she can't be angry; just sad.
    B. The letter tells how worried her parents are.
    C. The letter tells that Angel is being moved to a different museum.
    D. The letter says the mystery has already been solved.

10. Who does Mrs. Frankweiler call while the children are waiting to see her?
    A. The police
    B. Saxonberg
    C. The children's parents
    D. The museum

11. Why doesn't Claudia want to tell Mrs. Frankweiler where she and Jamie stayed all week?
    A. She wants to keep her secret.
    B. She wants to keep her bargaining power.
    C. She is afraid that telling will mean her trip is over.
    D. All of the above.

12. What are the terms of Mrs. Frankweiler's bargain regarding the secret of Angel?
    A. She will tell them the secret of Angel if the children will help her get Angel back.
    B. She will give the children 1 hour to find Angel's secret, and they will tell her the details of their week.
    C. She will tell them the secret of Angel if they will come and visit her whenever they can.
    D. She will give the children 1 hour to find the secret of Angel, but then she will call the police to take them home.

13. What deal does Mrs. Frankweiler make with Jamie and Claudia?
    A. She will bequeath the proof of Angel's background to the children if they will keep it a secret until after she dies.
    B. If she can beat Jamie at "war," she will tell them the truth about Angel.
    C. She'll tell them a secret about their grandfather if they will keep her secret about Angel.
    D. She won't turn them in to the police if they will keep her secret.

Mixed-Up Files Multiple Choice Unit Test 1 Page 4

14. What discovery does Claudia make about human nature and secrets?
    A. When you have a secret, it's no fun unless someone else knows you have one.
    B. Secrets are nothing but trouble.
    C. It isn't human nature to keep secrets; they have to be told.

15. How is Saxonberg connected to the children?
    A. He is in charge of their trust funds.
    B. He is the museum curator who overlooked their staying at the Metropolitan.
    C. He is their grandfather.
    D. He is Mrs. Frankweiler's driver who took them home.
    D. Secrets can be hurtful because human nature is to use secrets as bargaining power.

Mixed-Up Files Multiple Choice Unit Test 1 Page 5

III. Quotations
   Match the word or phrase to the quote.

A. statue
B. magic
C. mystery
D. beauty of the art
E. search
F. learn more about the statue
G. learn one new thing every day
H. learn about everything in the museum
I. result
J. secret
K. learning

1. "Claudia had found the article about the statue too easily. She didn't even look at the first section of the paper. I keep telling you that often the _____ proves more profitable than the goal. Keep that in mind when you're looking for something in my files" (61).

2. "…Michelangelo? I truly believe that this name has magic even now; the best kind of magic because it comes from true greatness. Claudia sensed it as she again stood in the line. The mystery only intrigued her; the _____ trapped her." (65).

3. "She would solve its _____; and it, in turn, would do something important to her, though what this was, she didn't quite know" (65).

4. "Claudia said, "But, Mrs. Frankweiler, you should want to _____. We did even at the museum."

5. "'I need having the _____ more than I need the money,' I told him. I knew that Claudia understood. Jamie looked puzzled." (148)

Mixed-Up Files Multiple Choice Unit Test 1 Page 6

IV. Vocabulary - Match the correct definitions to the words.

___ 1. THEATRICS   A. To look carefully, especially with narrowed eyes
___ 2. COUNTERED   B. To walk without picking up one's feet
___ 3. BROWSING   C. Prevented a person from speaking, especially in public
___ 4. DECEASED   D. An afternoon performance of a play, usually with cheaper seats than the evening performance
___ 5. DRIZZLE   E. A mixture of several unrelated things
___ 6. MUZZLED   F. Precise and correct
___ 7. ACCUSTOMED   G. Display of false and exaggerated emotion
___ 8. VETO   H. Extremely poor individuals
___ 9. IMPOSTER   I. Urged
___10. CHAUFFEUR   J. Gave something to somebody as his or her share of what is available
___11. ACCURATE   K. To say something that contradicts what someone else has said
___12. MONOTONY   L. Boredom that comes from doing the same thing over and over
___13. MATINEE   M. Someone who pretends to be someone he is not
___14. PAUPERS   N. Elaborately or elegantly decorated
___15. ASCENDED   O. Dead
___16. PEER   P. Bodies of people that have been embalmed and wrapped in cloth, as was the custom in ancient Egypt
___17. MEDIOCRE   Q. Complaining, especially when using harsh language
___18. SHUFFLING   R. Looking around in a leisurely manner
___19. ORNATELY   S. Went upward
___20. ALLOTTED   T. A king of ancient Egypt
___21. HODGEPODGE   U. Driver
___22. PROMPTED   V. To rain lightly
___23. MUMMIES   W. To exercise the right to reject something
___24. SCOLDING   X. Become used to a certain thing or way of doing things
___25. PHARAOH   Y. Adequate, but not very good

MULTIPLE CHOICE UNIT TEST 2
From the Mixed-Up Files of Mrs. Basil E. Frankweiler

I. Matching

___ 1. ANGEL   A. Place Claudia and Jamie go to research Michelangelo
___ 2. MET   B. Being away from home is not making Claudia and Jamie ___.
___ 3. LAUNDRY   C. Card game Jamie and Bruce play for money.
___ 4. JAMIE   D. Author of From The Mixed Up Files of Mrs. Basil E. Frankweiler
___ 5. PILLOW   E. The secret answer was found in the Bologna, ___ file.
___ 6. FARMINGTON   F. Mrs. Frankweiler asks Parks to bring her one.
___ 7. CLAUDIA   G. Town where Mrs. Frankweiler lives
___ 8. MOTHER   H. Claudia wanted to return home this way.
___ 9. SHELDON   I. He plays cards with Jamie on the school bus.
___10. TAXI   J. Playing cards and the fountain are sources of this.
___11. STATUE   K. Claudia places Jamie's instructions for running away here.
___12. FOUNTAIN   L. The statue with a secret.
___13. ITALY   M. Claudia and Jamie run out of clean ___.
___14. LIBRARY   N. Angel left three rings with an
___15. U. N.   O. She plans to run away.
___16. BRUCE   P. Short for The Metropolitan Museum of Art
___17. MONEY   Q. How Claudia and Jamie travel to Farmington, Connecticut
___18. MIRROR   R. Claudia sends for a rebate from this type of company.
___19. DIFFERENT   S. Place Claudia and Jamie bathe
___20. CEREAL   T. Claudia and Jamie take a tour of the ___.
___21. HOMESICK   U. Impossible thing Mrs. Frankweiler would like to be
___22. VELVET   V. He makes extra money gambling at cards.
___23. ROLLS   W. Jamie suggests fingerprinting this for clues.
___24. KONIGSBURG   X. Mrs. Frankweiler's driver
___25. WAR   Y. The children are driven home in a ___ Royce.

Mixed-Up Files Multiple Choice Unit Test 2 Page 2

II. Multiple Choice

1. How does Jamie make extra money?
    A. He walks the neighborhood dogs.
    B. He mows grass.
    C. He works for his grandfather.
    D. He gambles playing cards.

2. Why does Claudia suggest they skip Fifth Avenue?
    A. She is afraid.
    B. She is tired.
    C. She would be tempted to buy things.
    D. It is too far out of their way.

3. What do Claudia and Jamie do until 5:30 PM on their first day at the museum?
    A. Eat hot dogs from a street vendor
    B. Walk up and down Fifth Avenue
    C. Hide in the restrooms
    D. Hide behind a large statue in the lobby

4. How does Claudia plan to focus their learning at the museum?
    A. They will choose one painting from one gallery each day.
    B. They will learn about the museum's featured item each day.
    C. They will focus on Michelangelo and "Angel."
    D. They will follow a tour brochure they found.

5. How do Claudia and Jamie divide their research project?
    A. Claudia looks for books; Jamie checks the Internet
    B. Claudia looks in A-M; Jamie looks in N-Z.
    C. Claudia looks up Michelangelo; Jamie looks up Angel.
    D. Claudia reads reference books; Jamie looks in picture books.

6. Describe Claudia's and Jamie's discussion about homesickness.
    A. Claudia tells Jamie to be more "grown up," that homesickness is for babies.
    B. Jamie and Claudia are both homesick and decide that they should go home soon.
    C. They decide they're not homesick because they are more sure of themselves and better trained.
    D. Claudia is too busy to be homesick; she really wants to find out about Michelangelo. Jamie, on the other hand, is very homesick and wishes she would just give up and go home.

Mixed-Up Files Multiple Choice Unit Test 2 Page 3

7. What conclusion do Claudia and Jamie draw after looking at the velvet?
    A. It was originally commissioned for an Olympic event.
    B. It was stolen.
    C. It was created by Michelangelo.
    D. It was created by someone whose name began with "W."

8. How does Claudia use the encounter in the mastaba to her advantage?
    A. She finds a good place to hide.
    B. She overhears two knowledgeable museum patrons talking about Angel.
    C. She is able to have Jamie deliver a letter to the museum officials without giving away his identity.
    D. She gets some of Jamie's friends to sneak them some food.

9. Why isn't Claudia ready to go home after receiving the letter from the museum officials?
    A. She hasn't heard from her parents.
    B. She hasn't seen enough of the city on her own.
    C. She hasn't accomplished anything.
    D. She hasn't gotten over being angry.

10. How do the children spend the last of their money?
    A. Lunch
    B. Taxi fare and tip
    C. Newspaper
    D. Bus fare

11. What secret does Jamie Share with Mrs. Frankweiler?
    A. That he and Claudia have been staying at the Metropolitan Museum
    B. That Angel has Michelangelo's stonemason's mark on the bottom
    C. His method of cheating at cards
    D. That he and Claudia have been taking money from the fountain

12. What do Claudia and Jamie find in the file labeled "Bologna, Italy"?
    A. The history of the first bologna sandwich
    B. Money
    C. Italian notes with Michelangelo's signature on them.
    D. Proof that Michelangelo did create Angel

13. What is the one "impossible" thing that Mrs. Frankweiler would like to experience?
    A. Space flight
    B. A chance to talk with Michelangelo
    C. Motherhood
    D. Time travel

Mixed-Up Files Multiple Choice Unit Test 2 Page 4

14. What do the children plan to do every time they save enough money?
    A. Re-visit the Metropolitan
    B. Go to New York
    C. Buy a piece of art
    D. Visit Mrs. Frankweiler

15. What secret does Mrs. Frankweiler keep from Claudia and Jamie?
    A. She is over a hundred years old.
    B. She and their grandfather are engaged.
    C. She once met one of Michelangelo's direct descendants in Italy.
    D. Saxonberg has been her lawyer for over 40 years.

Mixed-Up Files Multiple Choice Unit Test 2 Page 5

III. Quotations
   Match the word or phrase to the quote.

A. learning
B. result
C. search
D. beauty of the art
E. mystery
F. learn about everything in the museum
G. learn one new thing every day
H. learn more about the statue
I. magic
J. secret
K. statue

1. "Claudia had found the article about the statue too easily. She didn't even look at the first section of the paper. I keep telling you that often the _____ proves more profitable than the goal. Keep that in mind when you're looking for something in my files" (61).

2. "…Michelangelo? I truly believe that this name has magic even now; the best kind of magic because it comes from true greatness. Claudia sensed it as she again stood in the line. The mystery only intrigued her; the _____ trapped her." (65).

3. "She would solve its _____; and it, in turn, would do something important to her, though what this was, she didn't quite know" (65).

4. "Claudia said, "But, Mrs. Frankweiler, you should want to _____. We did even at the museum."

5. "'I need having the _____ more than I need the money,' I told him. I knew that Claudia understood. Jamie looked puzzled." (148)

Mixed-Up Files Multiple Choice Unit Test 2 Page 6

IV. Vocabulary - Match the correct definitions to the words.

___ 1. THEATRICS A. The act of complimenting someone for the purpose of getting something

___ 2. HODGEPODGE B. Complaining, especially when using harsh language

___ 3. DESCENDING C. Revealed

___ 4. IMPOSTER D. Pointed someone in a particular direction

___ 5. ADVISED E. Precise and correct

___ 6. BAROQUE F. Made a realistic copy of

___ 7. PAUPERS G. Someone who pretends to be someone he is not

___ 8. EMERGE H. To appear

___ 9. ATTRIBUTING I. A mixture of several unrelated things

___ 10. COMPLEMENTED J. To say something that contradicts what someone else has said

___ 11. DISCLOSING K. Something completed something else, or made it near perfect

___ 12. SMUG L. Totally absorbed in doing or thinking about something else

___ 13. DELINQUENT M. Display of false and exaggerated emotion

___ 14. COUNTERED N. Recommended

___ 15. ACCURATE O. Conceited

___ 16. ORTHOPEDIC P. Coming down

___ 17. STEALTHILY Q. Secretively or cunningly

___ 18. COUNTERFEITED R. An ornamental style of European art (mid-16th to early 18th centuries)

___ 19. SCOLDING S. Giving credit to a person for a particular piece of art or work of literature

___ 20. DIRECTED T. Revealing or telling about

___ 21. PREOCCUPIED U. Extremely poor individuals

___ 22. EXPOSED V. To look carefully, especially with narrowed eyes

___ 23. FLATTERY W. Relating to disorders of the bones, joints, ligaments, or muscles

___ 24. SHEPHERDED X. Guided a group of people or animals

___ 25. PEER Y. A young person who has broken the law

ANSWER SHEET FOR THE MULTIPLE CHOICE UNIT TESTS
From the Mixed-Up Files of Mrs. Basil E. Frankweiler

	Matching	Multiple Choice	Quotes	Vocabulary
1				
2				
3				
4				
5				
6				
7				
8				
9				
10				
11				
12				
13				
14				
15				
16				
17				
18				
19				
20				
21				
22				
23				
24				
25				

ANSWER KEY MULTIPLE CHOICE UNIT TEST 1
From the Mixed-Up Files of Mrs. Basil E. Frankweiler

	Matching	Multiple Choice	Quotes	Vocabulary
1	A	C	E	G
2	J	C	B	K
3	K	A	C	R
4	N	B	G	O
5	H	A	J	V
6	L	D		C
7	R	C		X
8	Q	A		W
9	S	A		M
10	M	B		U
11	U	A		F
12	V	B		L
13	W	A		D
14	X	A		H
15	E	C		S
16	T			A
17	F			Y
18	O			B
19	C			N
20	G			J
21	Y			E
22	P			I
23	B			P
24	D			Q
25	I			T

ANSWER KEY MULTIPLE CHOICE UNIT TEST 2
From the Mixed-Up Files of Mrs. Basil E. Frankweiler

	Matching	Multiple Choice	Quotes	Vocabulary
1	L	D	C	M
2	P	C	I	I
3	M	C	E	P
4	V	C	G	G
5	K	D	J	N
6	G	C		R
7	O	C		U
8	U	C		H
9	X	C		S
10	Q	B		K
11	W	A		T
12	S	D		O
13	E	C		Y
14	A	D		J
15	T	D		R
16	I			W
17	J			Q
18	F			F
19	H			B
20	R			D
21	B			L
22	N			C
23	Y			A
24	D			X
25	C			

UNIT RESOURCE MATERIALS

BULLETIN BOARD IDEAS
From the Mixed-Up Files of Mrs. Basil E. Frankweiler

1. Save one corner of the board for the best of students' *Mixed-Up Files* writing assignments.

2. Take one of the word search puzzles from the extra activities packet and, with a marker, copy it over in a large size on the bulletin board. Write the clue words to find to one side. Invite students prior to and after class to find the words and circle them on the bulletin board.

3. Write several of the most significant quotations from the book onto the board on brightly colored paper.

4. Make a bulletin board listing the vocabulary words for this unit. As you complete sections of the novel and discuss the vocabulary for each section, write the definitions on the bulletin board. (If your board is one students face frequently, it will help them learn the words.)

5. Post information and photographs about New York City and its main attractions. Invite students to add to the display throughout the unit.

6. Post photographs of The Metropolitan Museum of Art and its major holdings. Highlight special exhibits currently on display at the museum. Similarly, you may choose to feature a museum closer to your school.

7. Title a display "New York City: Then and Now." Post illustrations or artifacts (tokens, tickets, passes, etc.) that existed when the novel was first published in 1972 alongside more modern versions.

8. Have students bring in and post photographs of themselves with their families or siblings.

9. Track an on-going news item or post articles from various newspapers as the unit progresses. Students may bring in articles as well. Similarly, students may choose to create headlines or news articles based on events from the novel to post on the bulletin board.

10. Post an enlarged map of The Metropolitan Museum of Art on the board. Assign a colored string to each day of Claudia's and Jamie's journey, and have the class trace the day's journey with the string. You could also post maps and mark their entire trip–from home through New York, to Mrs. Frankweiler's house, and home again.

11. Make a bulletin board about The Hero's Journey. Enlarge the explanation of each step and put it on brightly colored paper. Make arrows between the steps. Use the board to help discuss the Hero's Journey theme in *Mixed-Up Files*.

12. Set up the bulletin board to resemble a *Jeopardy* game board. Students could be responsible for creating the categories, questions, and answers.

EXTRA ACTIVITIES
From the Mixed-Up Files of Mrs. Basil E. Frankweiler

One of the difficulties in teaching a novel is that all students don't read at the same speed. One student who likes to read may take the book home and finish it in a day or two. Sometimes a few students finish the in-class assignments early. The problem, then, is finding suitable extra activities for students.

One thing that seems to help is to keep a little library in the classroom. For this unit on *Mixed-Up Files*, you might check out the following works from the school library:

    Items relating to any of the topics listed in the non-fiction assignment
    Newspapers
    Books, magazines, or articles about art, art history, The Met or other museums
    Books, magazines, or articles about ancient Egypt
    Books, magazines, or articles about public transportation

    Other novels by E. L. Konigsburg, including:
        Jennifer, Hecate, MacBeth, William McKinley, and Me, Elizabeth
        Outcasts of 19 Shuyler Place
        The View From Saturday
        Silent to the Bone
        The Second Mrs. Gioconda

Other things you may keep on hand are puzzles. We have made some relating directly to *Mixed-Up Files* for you. Feel free to duplicate them for your students to use.

Some students may like to draw. You might devise a contest or allow some extra-credit grade for students who draw characters or scenes from *Mixed-Up Files*. This is particularly appropriate for the character study portion of the unit. Note, too, that if the students do not want to keep their drawings you may pick up some extra bulletin board materials this way. If you have a contest and you supply the prize (a CD or something like that perhaps), you could, possibly, make the drawing itself a non-returnable entry fee.

The pages which follow contain games, puzzles and worksheets. The keys, when appropriate, immediately follow the puzzle or worksheet. There are two main groups of activities: one group for the unit; that is, generally relating to the *Mixed-Up Files* text, and another group of activities related strictly to the *Mixed-Up Files* vocabulary.

Directions for these games, puzzles and worksheets are self-explanatory. The object here is to provide you with extra materials you may use in any way you choose.

MORE ACTIVITIES - *Mixed-Up Files*

1. Have students work together to make a time line chronology of the events in the story. Take a large piece of construction paper and on one wall (or however you can physically arrange it in your room) and make the events of the story along it. Students may want to add drawings or cut-out pictures to represent the events (as well as written statements).

2. Have students design a book cover (front and back and inside flaps) for *The Mixed-Up Files*.

3. Have students design a bulletin board (ready to be put up, not just sketched) for *The Mixed-Up Files*.

4. Have students create a chapter of the book written in the first person point-of-view by Jamie.

5. Have students choose one chapter of the book (with sufficient dialogue) to rewrite as a play. In conjunction with this assignment, have students write a composition explaining the difficulties they encountered in changing from one written form to another.

6. Have each student choose an artist or a particular piece of artwork to research. Students could each then create a page for an art book. Someone could write the introduction and table of contents. Or each person could make a section of a multimedia or Power Point presentation.

7. Host *A Day At The Museum*. Each person could bring in a picture, a piece of artwork, or an antique from home. Each piece should have a descriptive paragraph to go with it for the display. After all the items are set up, students could view all of the items. Then, they could discuss them, write about them, vote for and/or award prizes for the oldest, the most unusual, the funniest, the best-preserved, the most original, etc. You can think of lots of categories so many prizes will be awarded. In conjunction with this event, you could host a small reception. It could all get quite elaborate, or you could keep it simple, depending on your students, your time frame, and your energy level.

8. Let your students try their hands at sculpting Angel (or something else of their choice)! Depending on what materials are readily available in your area, you could have students bring in a chunk of wood, a big thing of clay, or you could mix up big batches of really stiff dough.

9. Do a class or group writing project in which students write the scene when Claudia and Jamie return home and greet their parents.

Mixed Up Files of Mrs. Basil E. Frankweiler Word List

No.	Word	Clue/Definition
1.	ADOPT	The children plan to secretly _____ Mrs. Frankweiler.
2.	ANGEL	The statue with a secret.
3.	ATTORNEY	Occupation of Claudia and Jamie's grandfather.
4.	BRILLIANT	Jamie flatters Claudia by calling her ____.
5.	BRUCE	He plays cards with Jamie on the school bus.
6.	BUS	Claudia and Jamie skip school by hiding in the school _____.
7.	CEREAL	Claudia sends for a rebate from this type of company.
8.	CLAUDIA	She plans to run away.
9.	COINS	Jamie is carrying $24.43 worth of these in his pockets.
10.	DIFFERENT	Claudia wanted to return home this way.
11.	FARMINGTON	Town where Mrs. Frankweiler lives
12.	FIFTH	Strolling down _____ Avenue may cause Claudia to shop.
13.	FOUNTAIN	Place Claudia and Jamie bathe
14.	FRANKWEILER	Sold Angel to the Metropolitan Museum of Art
15.	HOMESICK	Being away from home is not making Claudia and Jamie ____.
16.	ITALY	The secret answer was found in the Bologna, ____ file.
17.	JAMIE	He makes extra money gambling at cards.
18.	KONIGSBURG	Author of From The Mixed Up Files of Mrs. Basil E. Frankweiler
19.	LAUNDRY	Claudia and Jamie run out of clean ____.
20.	LIBRARY	Place Claudia and Jamie go to research Michelangelo
21.	MET	Short for The Metropolitan Museum of Art
22.	MICHELANGELO	He created Angel.
23.	MIRROR	Mrs. Frankweiler asks Parks to bring her one.
24.	MONEY	Playing cards and the fountain are sources of this.
25.	MOTHER	Impossible thing Mrs. Frankweiler would like to be
26.	MUSEUM	Place Claudia and Jamie run away to
27.	ONE	Number of hours the kids have to find the secret.
28.	PARKS	Mrs. Frankweiler's butler
29.	PILLOW	Claudia places Jamie's instructions for running away here.
30.	PLANNING	Claudia's special talent
31.	ROLLS	The children are driven home in a ____ Royce.
32.	SARCOPHAGUS	Place Claudia hides her violin case
33.	SAXONBERG	Mrs. Frankweiler's lawyer
34.	SECRET	Claudia and Mrs. Frankweiler both like keeping these.
35.	SHELDON	Mrs. Frankweiler's driver
36.	SKETCH	Mrs. Frankweiler plans to bequeath this to the children.
37.	SMELLS	Claudia treasures good, clean ____.
38.	SONNET	One was written on the back of a sketch of Angel.
39.	STATUE	Jamie suggests fingerprinting this for clues.
40.	TAXI	How Claudia and Jamie travel to Farmington, Connecticut
41.	TRAIN	Claudia finds a _____ ticket in the wastebasket.
42.	UN	Claudia and Jamie take a tour of the ____.
43.	VELVET	Angel left three rings with an
44.	VIOLIN	Claudia uses her ____ case as a suitcase.
45.	WAR	Card game Jamie and Bruce play for money.

WORD SEARCH - Mixed Up Files of Mrs. Basil E. Frankweiler

```
B R I L L I A N T A T T O R N E Y P X X
Q S H B W G R U B S G I N O K L D I S H
D F R A N K W E I L E R D M N A Z L P H
I R X Q G Q F B F V C L Z I F U R L G D
F H F R P E K H C Y E Q D C O N B O R W
F S P C I L S R T H Z V Q H U D M W E V
E H E M P D A E S V T Y Z E N R U H B H
R R A C V J N N N H R P B L T Y S K N J
E J F P R N Q K N B A G S A A C E R O J
N J B Z O E C I R I I Z L N I O U W X J
T E M S K E T C H J N O T G N I M R A F
E Z B M Y A J X H I U G S E L N G I S R
U Q P Y L F M B L O D V J L Y S D F F K
T F F Y V I H O C M M Q T O K U Z J T S
A Y R A R B I L M O N E Y P A R K S R Y
T D T R R V P T J O V S S L C N F B V C
S N O X Z Z C P Z L T C C I T T G P Q C
Z R Z P H L V V E B E H S R C A R E N W
S F I F T H S V Y R T C E M O K X L L K
B Q X J V U Y Z E U R F S R E L H I R Z
C B M H B Q Y A J C G L F W J L L L Y F
K G T F H K L P T E L W F Q T X L S C B
B M T H Q S D S A R C O P H A G U S N S
```

ADOPT	FOUNTAIN	MOTHER	SMELLS
ANGEL	FRANKWEILER	MUSEUM	SONNET
ATTORNEY	HOMESICK	ONE	STATUE
BRILLIANT	ITALY	PARKS	TAXI
BRUCE	JAMIE	PILLOW	TRAIN
BUS	KONIGSBURG	PLANNING	UN
CEREAL	LAUNDRY	ROLLS	VELVET
CLAUDIA	LIBRARY	SARCOPHAGUS	VIOLIN
COINS	MET	SAXONBERG	WAR
DIFFERENT	MICHELANGELO	SECRET	
FARMINGTON	MIRROR	SHELDON	
FIFTH	MONEY	SKETCH	

WORD SEARCH ANSWER KEY - Mixed Up Files of Mrs. Basil E. Frankweiler

ADOPT	FOUNTAIN	MOTHER	SMELLS
ANGEL	FRANKWEILER	MUSEUM	SONNET
ATTORNEY	HOMESICK	ONE	STATUE
BRILLIANT	ITALY	PARKS	TAXI
BRUCE	JAMIE	PILLOW	TRAIN
BUS	KONIGSBURG	PLANNING	UN
CEREAL	LAUNDRY	ROLLS	VELVET
CLAUDIA	LIBRARY	SARCOPHAGUS	VIOLIN
COINS	MET	SAXONBERG	WAR
DIFFERENT	MICHELANGELO	SECRET	
FARMINGTON	MIRROR	SHELDON	
FIFTH	MONEY	SKETCH	

CROSSWORD - Mixed Up Files of Mrs. Basil E. Frankweiler

Across
1. Jamie is carrying $24.43 worth of these in his pockets.
3. Town where Mrs. Frankweiler lives
6. Claudia sends for a rebate from this type of company.
8. Mrs. Frankweiler's butler
9. Strolling down _____ Avenue may cause Claudia to shop.
10. Card game Jamie and Bruce play for money.
12. The children plan to secretly _____ Mrs. Frankweiler.
13. Jamie flatters Claudia by calling her ____.
15. Claudia and Jamie run out of clean ____.
17. Short for The Metropolitan Museum of Art
18. Claudia and Jamie take a tour of the ____.
19. Claudia and Jamie skip school by hiding in the school _____.

Down
2. Number of hours the kids have to find the secret.
4. Mrs. Frankweiler asks Parks to bring her one.
5. How Claudia and Jamie travel to Farmington, Connecticut
6. She plans to run away.
7. Occupation of Claudia and Jamie's grandfather.
11. The secret answer was found in the Bologna, ____ file.
12. The statue with a secret.
13. He plays cards with Jamie on the school bus.
14. Claudia finds a _____ ticket in the wastebasket.
16. The children are driven home in a ____ Royce.

CROSSWORD ANSWER KEY - Mixed Up Files of Mrs. Basil E. Frankweiler

	1 C	2 O	I	N	S		3 F	A	R	4 M	I	N	G	5 T	O	N	
		N								I				A			
	6 C	E	R	E	7 A	L		8 P	A	R	K	S		X			
		L			T				R				9 F	I	F	T	H
10 W	A	R			T		11 I		O								
			12 A	D	O	P	T		13 B	R	I	L	L	I	A	N	14 T
			N		R		A		R								R
			I		G		N		15 L	A	U	N	16 D	R	Y		A
			A		E		E		Y		C		O				I
					L		Y			17 M	E	T	L			18 U	N
													L				
										19 B	U	S					

Across
1. Jamie is carrying $24.43 worth of these in his pockets.
3. Town where Mrs. Frankweiler lives
6. Claudia sends for a rebate from this type of company.
8. Mrs. Frankweiler's butler
9. Strolling down _____ Avenue may cause Claudia to shop.
10. Card game Jamie and Bruce play for money.
12. The children plan to secretly _____ Mrs. Frankweiler.
13. Jamie flatters Claudia by calling her ____.
15. Claudia and Jamie run out of clean ____.
17. Short for The Metropolitan Museum of Art
18. Claudia and Jamie take a tour of the ____.
19. Claudia and Jamie skip school by hiding in the school _____.

Down
2. Number of hours the kids have to find the secret.
4. Mrs. Frankweiler asks Parks to bring her one.
5. How Claudia and Jamie travel to Farmington, Connecticut
6. She plans to run away.
7. Occupation of Claudia and Jamie's grandfather.
11. The secret answer was found in the Bologna, ____ file.
12. The statue with a secret.
13. He plays cards with Jamie on the school bus.
14. Claudia finds a _____ ticket in the wastebasket.
16. The children are driven home in a ____ Royce.

152

MATCHING 1 - Mixed Up Files of Mrs. Basil E. Frankweiler

___ 1. DIFFERENT   A. Claudia places Jamie's instructions for running away here.

___ 2. SMELLS   B. Short for The Metropolitan Museum of Art

___ 3. PILLOW   C. Number of hours the kids have to find the secret.

___ 4. MICHELANGELO   D. Claudia and Mrs. Frankweiler both like keeping these.

___ 5. MET   E. The secret answer was found in the Bologna, ____ file.

___ 6. ITALY   F. Claudia sends for a rebate from this type of company.

___ 7. ONE   G. Angel left three rings with an

___ 8. ROLLS   H. The children are driven home in a ____ Royce.

___ 9. LIBRARY   I. Claudia wanted to return home this way.

___ 10. CLAUDIA   J. Claudia and Jamie take a tour of the ____.

___ 11. SECRET   K. He plays cards with Jamie on the school bus.

___ 12. JAMIE   L. Place Claudia and Jamie bathe

___ 13. UN   M. She plans to run away.

___ 14. FOUNTAIN   N. Place Claudia and Jamie go to research Michelangelo

___ 15. CEREAL   O. Place Claudia and Jamie run away to

___ 16. BRILLIANT   P. Place Claudia hides her violin case

___ 17. PARKS   Q. Claudia treasures good, clean ____.

___ 18. VELVET   R. Mrs. Frankweiler's butler

___ 19. ANGEL   S. He makes extra money gambling at cards.

___ 20. MUSEUM   T. Jamie flatters Claudia by calling her ____.

___ 21. TRAIN   U. The statue with a secret.

___ 22. COINS   V. He created Angel.

___ 23. SARCOPHAGUS   W. Mrs. Frankweiler plans to bequeath this to the children.

___ 24. BRUCE   X. Claudia finds a ____ ticket in the wastebasket.

___ 25. SKETCH   Y. Jamie is carrying $24.43 worth of these in his pockets.

MATCHING 1 ANSWER KEY - Mixed Up Files of Mrs. Basil E. Frankweiler

I - 1. DIFFERENT	A.	Claudia places Jamie's instructions for running away here.
Q - 2. SMELLS	B.	Short for The Metropolitan Museum of Art
A - 3. PILLOW	C.	Number of hours the kids have to find the secret.
V - 4. MICHELANGELO	D.	Claudia and Mrs. Frankweiler both like keeping these.
B - 5. MET	E.	The secret answer was found in the Bologna, ____ file.
E - 6. ITALY	F.	Claudia sends for a rebate from this type of company.
C - 7. ONE	G.	Angel left three rings with an
H - 8. ROLLS	H.	The children are driven home in a ____ Royce.
N - 9. LIBRARY	I.	Claudia wanted to return home this way.
M -10. CLAUDIA	J.	Claudia and Jamie take a tour of the ____.
D -11. SECRET	K.	He plays cards with Jamie on the school bus.
S -12. JAMIE	L.	Place Claudia and Jamie bathe
J -13. UN	M.	She plans to run away.
L -14. FOUNTAIN	N.	Place Claudia and Jamie go to research Michelangelo
F -15. CEREAL	O.	Place Claudia and Jamie run away to
T -16. BRILLIANT	P.	Place Claudia hides her violin case
R -17. PARKS	Q.	Claudia treasures good, clean ____.
G -18. VELVET	R.	Mrs. Frankweiler's butler
U -19. ANGEL	S.	He makes extra money gambling at cards.
O -20. MUSEUM	T.	Jamie flatters Claudia by calling her ____.
X -21. TRAIN	U.	The statue with a secret.
Y -22. COINS	V.	He created Angel.
P -23. SARCOPHAGUS	W.	Mrs. Frankweiler plans to bequeath this to the children.
K -24. BRUCE	X.	Claudia finds a _____ ticket in the wastebasket.
W 25. SKETCH	Y.	Jamie is carrying $24.43 worth of these in his pockets.

MATCHING 2 - Mixed Up Files of Mrs. Basil E. Frankweiler

___ 1. FARMINGTON   A. The children plan to secretly _____ Mrs. Frankweiler.

___ 2. SAXONBERG   B. Angel left three rings with an

___ 3. ITALY   C. Claudia treasures good, clean ____.

___ 4. MET   D. Sold Angel to the Metropolitan Museum of Art

___ 5. TAXI   E. Claudia finds a _____ ticket in the wastebasket.

___ 6. MUSEUM   F. Playing cards and the fountain are sources of this.

___ 7. CEREAL   G. Place Claudia and Jamie go to research Michelangelo

___ 8. PILLOW   H. Card game Jamie and Bruce play for money.

___ 9. UN   I. Claudia sends for a rebate from this type of company.

___10. JAMIE   J. Mrs. Frankweiler plans to bequeath this to the children.

___11. VELVET   K. He makes extra money gambling at cards.

___12. SMELLS   L. How Claudia and Jamie travel to Farmington, Connecticut

___13. PLANNING   M. Claudia places Jamie's instructions for running away here.

___14. MONEY   N. Mrs. Frankweiler's lawyer

___15. SKETCH   O. Short for The Metropolitan Museum of Art

___16. ADOPT   P. Mrs. Frankweiler's driver

___17. WAR   Q. Place Claudia and Jamie run away to

___18. LIBRARY   R. Claudia uses her ____ case as a suitcase.

___19. FRANKWEILER   S. Claudia and Jamie take a tour of the ____.

___20. VIOLIN   T. He plays cards with Jamie on the school bus.

___21. MIRROR   U. The secret answer was found in the Bologna, ____ file.

___22. BRUCE   V. Place Claudia hides her violin case

___23. SHELDON   W. Claudia's special talent

___24. TRAIN   X. Mrs. Frankweiler asks Parks to bring her one.

___25. SARCOPHAGUS   Y. Town where Mrs. Frankweiler lives

MATCHING 2 ANSWER KEY - Mixed Up Files of Mrs. Basil E. Frankweiler

Y - 1. FARMINGTON	A.	The children plan to secretly _____ Mrs. Frankweiler.
N - 2. SAXONBERG	B.	Angel left three rings with an
U - 3. ITALY	C.	Claudia treasures good, clean ____.
O - 4. MET	D.	Sold Angel to the Metropolitan Museum of Art
L - 5. TAXI	E.	Claudia finds a _____ ticket in the wastebasket.
Q - 6. MUSEUM	F.	Playing cards and the fountain are sources of this.
I - 7. CEREAL	G.	Place Claudia and Jamie go to research Michelangelo
M - 8. PILLOW	H.	Card game Jamie and Bruce play for money.
S - 9. UN	I.	Claudia sends for a rebate from this type of company.
K -10. JAMIE	J.	Mrs. Frankweiler plans to bequeath this to the children.
B -11. VELVET	K.	He makes extra money gambling at cards.
C -12. SMELLS	L.	How Claudia and Jamie travel to Farmington, Connecticut
W 13. PLANNING	M.	Claudia places Jamie's instructions for running away here.
F -14. MONEY	N.	Mrs. Frankweiler's lawyer
J -15. SKETCH	O.	Short for The Metropolitan Museum of Art
A -16. ADOPT	P.	Mrs. Frankweiler's driver
H -17. WAR	Q.	Place Claudia and Jamie run away to
G -18. LIBRARY	R.	Claudia uses her ____ case as a suitcase.
D -19. FRANKWEILER	S.	Claudia and Jamie take a tour of the ____.
R -20. VIOLIN	T.	He plays cards with Jamie on the school bus.
X -21. MIRROR	U.	The secret answer was found in the Bologna, ____ file.
T -22. BRUCE	V.	Place Claudia hides her violin case
P -23. SHELDON	W.	Claudia's special talent
E -24. TRAIN	X.	Mrs. Frankweiler asks Parks to bring her one.
V -25. SARCOPHAGUS	Y.	Town where Mrs. Frankweiler lives

JUGGLE LETTER 1 - Mixed Up Files of Mrs. Basil E. Frankweiler

1. MAJIE = 1. _____
He makes extra money gambling at cards.

2. RFEEDFTNI = 2. _____
Claudia wanted to return home this way.

3. TEM = 3. _____
Short for The Metropolitan Museum of Art

4. MROTNGNIAF = 4. _____
Town where Mrs. Frankweiler lives

5. EVLVET = 5. _____
Angel left three rings with an

6. BLRIRYA = 6. _____
Place Claudia and Jamie go to research Michelangelo

7. NOANFITU = 7. _____
Place Claudia and Jamie bathe

8. NU = 8. _____
Claudia and Jamie take a tour of the ____.

9. ODNEHSL = 9. _____
Mrs. Frankweiler's driver

10. KLIAFWERNER =10. _____
Sold Angel to the Metropolitan Museum of Art

11. SAPRK =11. _____
Mrs. Frankweiler's butler

12. APURHSGASOC =12. _____
Place Claudia hides her violin case

13. YTLAI =13. _____
The secret answer was found in the Bologna, ____ file.

14. LANGE =14. _____
The statue with a secret.

15. LVINOI =15. _____
Claudia uses her ____ case as a suitcase.

16. TPODA =16. _____
   The children plan to secretly _____ Mrs. Frankweiler.

17. ESMUUM =17. _____
   Place Claudia and Jamie run away to

18. XTIA =18. _____
   How Claudia and Jamie travel to Farmington, Connecticut

19. OLLAEHCINEGM =19. _____
   He created Angel.

20. KCTSHE =20. _____
   Mrs. Frankweiler plans to bequeath this to the children.

21. OESNTN =21. _____
   One was written on the back of a sketch of Angel.

22. IOSCN =22. _____
   Jamie is carrying $24.43 worth of these in his pockets.

23. ATNILRLBI =23. _____
   Jamie flatters Claudia by calling her ____.

JUGGLE LETTER 1 ANSWER KEY - Mixed Up Files of Mrs. Basil E. Frankweiler

1. MAJIE = 1. JAMIE
He makes extra money gambling at cards.

2. RFEEDFTNI = 2. DIFFERENT
Claudia wanted to return home this way.

3. TEM = 3. MET
Short for The Metropolitan Museum of Art

4. MROTNGNIAF = 4. FARMINGTON
Town where Mrs. Frankweiler lives

5. EVLVET = 5. VELVET
Angel left three rings with an

6. BLRIRYA = 6. LIBRARY
Place Claudia and Jamie go to research Michelangelo

7. NOANFITU = 7. FOUNTAIN
Place Claudia and Jamie bathe

8. NU = 8. UN
Claudia and Jamie take a tour of the ____.

9. ODNEHSL = 9. SHELDON
Mrs. Frankweiler's driver

10. KLIAFWERNER =10. FRANKWEILER
Sold Angel to the Metropolitan Museum of Art

11. SAPRK =11. PARKS
Mrs. Frankweiler's butler

12. APURHSGASOC =12. SARCOPHAGUS
Place Claudia hides her violin case

13. YTLAI =13. ITALY
The secret answer was found in the Bologna, ____ file.

14. LANGE =14. ANGEL
The statue with a secret.

15. LVINOI =15. VIOLIN
Claudia uses her ____ case as a suitcase.

16. TPODA   =16. ADOPT
                    The children plan to secretly _____ Mrs. Frankweiler.

17. ESMUUM   =17. MUSEUM
                    Place Claudia and Jamie run away to

18. XTIA   =18. TAXI
                    How Claudia and Jamie travel to Farmington, Connecticut

19. OLLAEHCINEGM   =19. MICHELANGELO
                    He created Angel.

20. KCTSHE   =20. SKETCH
                    Mrs. Frankweiler plans to bequeath this to the children.

21. OESNTN   =21. SONNET
                    One was written on the back of a sketch of Angel.

22. IOSCN   =22. COINS
                    Jamie is carrying $24.43 worth of these in his pockets.

23. ATNILRLBI   =23. BRILLIANT
                    Jamie flatters Claudia by calling her _____.

JUGGLE LETTER 2 - Mixed Up Files of Mrs. Basil E. Frankweiler

1. REMOHT = 1. _____
   Impossible thing Mrs. Frankweiler would like to be

2. TEASTU = 2. _____
   Jamie suggests fingerprinting this for clues.

3. SLLOR = 3. _____
   The children are driven home in a ____ Royce.

4. IALGNNNP = 4. _____
   Claudia's special talent

5. EON = 5. _____
   Number of hours the kids have to find the secret.

6. UBS = 6. _____
   Claudia and Jamie skip school by hiding in the school _____.

7. ATNIR = 7. _____
   Claudia finds a_____ ticket in the wastebasket.

8. OBSXENRGA = 8. _____
   Mrs. Frankweiler's lawyer

9. LOWIPL = 9. _____
   Claudia places Jamie's instructions for running away here.

10. ELSMSL =10. _____
    Claudia treasures good, clean ____.

11. ESICKHOM =11. _____
    Being away from home is not making Claudia and Jamie ____.

12. CUBER =12. _____
    He plays cards with Jamie on the school bus.

13. EESCRT =13. _____
    Claudia and Mrs. Frankweiler both like keeping these.

14. ARW =14. _____
    Card game Jamie and Bruce play for money.

15. IUDALCA =15. _____
    She plans to run away.

16. RIORMR =16. _____
Mrs. Frankweiler asks Parks to bring her one.

17. YONEM =17. _____
Playing cards and the fountain are sources of this.

18. YRUANDL =18. _____
Claudia and Jamie run out of clean ____.

19. CELAER =19. _____
Claudia sends for a rebate from this type of company.

20. HTFIF =20. _____
Strolling down _____ Avenue may cause Claudia to shop.

21. RNATTEOY =21. _____
Occupation of Claudia and Jamie's grandfather.

22. GSBNIGUORK =22. _____
Author of From The Mixed Up Files of Mrs. Basil E. Frankweiler

JUGGLE LETTER 2 ANSWER KEY - Mixed Up Files of Mrs. Basil E. Frankweiler

1. REMOHT = 1. MOTHER
   Impossible thing Mrs. Frankweiler would like to be

2. TEASTU = 2. STATUE
   Jamie suggests fingerprinting this for clues.

3. SLLOR = 3. ROLLS
   The children are driven home in a ____ Royce.

4. IALGNNNP = 4. PLANNING
   Claudia's special talent

5. EON = 5. ONE
   Number of hours the kids have to find the secret.

6. UBS = 6. BUS
   Claudia and Jamie skip school by hiding in the school _____.

7. ATNIR = 7. TRAIN
   Claudia finds a _____ ticket in the wastebasket.

8. OBSXENRGA = 8. SAXONBERG
   Mrs. Frankweiler's lawyer

9. LOWIPL = 9. PILLOW
   Claudia places Jamie's instructions for running away here.

10. ELSMSL = 10. SMELLS
    Claudia treasures good, clean ____.

11. ESICKHOM = 11. HOMESICK
    Being away from home is not making Claudia and Jamie ____.

12. CUBER = 12. BRUCE
    He plays cards with Jamie on the school bus.

13. EESCRT = 13. SECRET
    Claudia and Mrs. Frankweiler both like keeping these.

14. ARW = 14. WAR
    Card game Jamie and Bruce play for money.

15. IUDALCA = 15. CLAUDIA
    She plans to run away.

16. RIORMR =16. MIRROR
Mrs. Frankweiler asks Parks to bring her one.

17. YONEM =17. MONEY
Playing cards and the fountain are sources of this.

18. YRUANDL =18. LAUNDRY
Claudia and Jamie run out of clean ____.

19. CELAER =19. CEREAL
Claudia sends for a rebate from this type of company.

20. HTFIF =20. FIFTH
Strolling down _____ Avenue may cause Claudia to shop.

21. RNATTEOY =21. ATTORNEY
Occupation of Claudia and Jamie's grandfather.

22. GSBNIGUORK =22. KONIGSBURG
Author of From The Mixed Up Files of Mrs. Basil E. Frankweiler

VOCABULARY RESOURCE MATERIALS

Mixed Up Files of Mrs. Basil E. Frankweiler Vocabulary Word List

No.	Word	Clue/Definition
1.	ABRASIONS	Areas of the skin that has been hurt by scraping
2.	ACCURATE	Precise and correct
3.	ACCUSTOMED	Become used to a certain thing or way of doing things
4.	ADVISED	Recommended
5.	ALLOTTED	Gave something to somebody as his or her share of what is available
6.	AMASSED	Collected over time until they form a large fund
7.	ASCENDED	Went upward
8.	ASSOCIATED	Connected to or having to do with
9.	ATTRIBUTING	Giving credit to a person for a particular piece of art or work of literature
10.	BAROQUE	An ornamental style of European art (mid-16th to early 18th centuries)
11.	BROWSING	Looking around in a leisurely manner
12.	CAPER	A light-hearted adventure or a dangerous illegal activity
13.	CHAUFFEUR	Driver
14.	CLAMPED	Held tightly over
15.	COMMOTION	Noisy activity or confusion
16.	COMPLEMENTED	Something completed something else, or made it close to perfect
17.	COUNTERED	To say something that contradicts what someone else has said
18.	COUNTERFEITED	Made a realistic copy of
19.	DECEASED	Dead
20.	DELINQUENT	A young person who has broken the law
21.	DESCENDING	Coming down
22.	DIRECTED	Pointed someone in a particular direction
23.	DISCLOSING	Revealing or telling about
24.	DISMALLY	In a depressing manner
25.	DISMISS	To officially release students from school
26.	DRIZZLE	To rain lightly
27.	EMERGE	To appear
28.	EXPOSED	Revealed
29.	FLATTERY	The act of complimenting someone for the purpose of getting something
30.	FOOTNOTES	An explanation at the bottom of a page giving further information about something in the text above
31.	HODGEPODGE	A mixture of several unrelated things
32.	HUMILITY	A feeling of modesty
33.	IMPOSTER	Someone who pretends to be someone he is not
34.	INJUSTICE	Unfair treatment
35.	INTRIGUED	To make someone very interested
36.	KEEN	Slang term for very cool
37.	LIBERTY	Freedom to think or act
38.	MAIMED	Affected with a severe and permanent injury
39.	MASTABA	An ancient Egyptian tomb with a flat base, sloping sides, and a flat roof
40.	MATINEE	An afternoon performance of a play, usually with cheaper seats than the evening performance
41.	MEDIOCRE	Adequate, but not very good
42.	MONOTONY	boredom that comes from doing the same thing over and over
43.	MUMMIES	Bodies of people that have been embalmed and wrapped in cloth, as was the custom in ancient Egypt
44.	MUTUAL	Shared
45.	MUZZLED	Prevented a person from speaking, especially in public

Mixed Up Files of Mrs. Basil E. Frankweiler Vocabulary Continued

No.	Word	Clue/Definition
46.	ORNATELY	Elaborately or elegantly decorated
47.	ORTHOPEDIC	Relating to disorders of the bones, joints, ligaments, or muscles
48.	PAUPERS	Extremely poor individuals
49.	PEER	To look carefully, especially with narrowed eyes
50.	PERSUADE	To convince or make someone believe something
51.	PHARAOH	A king of ancient Egypt
52.	PREOCCUPIED	Totally absorbed in doing or thinking about something else
53.	PROMPTED	Urged
54.	PUBLICITY	Public interest or knowledge
55.	PUNCTUATED	To end with emphasis
56.	QUARRIED	Obtained or gotten after much effort
57.	REGARD	To think of a person or thing in a particular way
58.	SARCOPHAGUS	An ancient stone or marble coffin
59.	SCOLDING	Complaining, especially when using harsh language
60.	SCOWLED	Made a facial expression characterized by drawing the eyebrows together in anger or displeasure
61.	SCREECHED	Made a loud, high-pitched sound
62.	SEEPED	Passed through an opening very slowly
63.	SHEPHERDED	Guided a group of people or animals
64.	SHRUNKEN	Characterized by a decrease in size
65.	SHUFFLING	To walk without picking up one's feet
66.	SMUG	Conceited
67.	STAMMERED	Spoke with many hesitations due to fear or strong emotion
68.	STEALTHILY	Secretively or cunningly
69.	STOWAWAY	Someone who hides on a traveling vessel in hopes of gaining passage without paying
70.	SUMMONED	Sent for someone to come
71.	THEATRICS	Display of false and exaggerated emotion
72.	TRANSPORTED	Moved someone or something from one place to another, especially in a vehicle
73.	TYRANNIES	Cruelties suffered at the hand of people in authority
74.	VENDOR	Someone who sells something
75.	VETO	To exercise the right to reject something

VOCABULARY WORD SEARCH - Mixed Up Files of Mrs. Basil E. Frankweiler

```
A Q U A R R I E D E M I A M S V P S D Z
C P B H Q W M E E M W R S P T P A U I B
C D Z J V L R B L U S G C R A U U M S P
U D R A G E R D W M C N E O M B P M M C
R K Z F T O E Y O M O I N M M L E O I R
A N G N W L A Y C I L D D P E I R N S X
T F U S Z B L X S E D N E T R C S E S N
E O I Z A L B R F S I E D E E I S D S Y
C N U T A A S E D L N C L D D T G R H S
G M S M R J A T E I G S T I O Y K I R G
D A S O J Z R S T B R E R W N W X Z U D
M I Q H L P C O T E J D A L P Q G Z N K
D U C E E F O P O R N W N W Q Y U L K L
E P Z D D P P M L T A J S E P V D E E I
S T E A L T H I L Y K R P M L K E E N J
I Y L U G O A E A D U M O E U S C J W T
V S A S A P G Z R E E N R R M G U D K E
D G M R M E U M F D O R T G A S X E X B
A Z A E V E S F I T E O E E T C A P E R
X H S P R R U O O X T D D I I L O M N M
P P S S S A C N D E G N C D N S F A F S
Q C E V H R Y J V T S E E P E D G L Z W
M F D C E M U T U A L V M D E Z K C Q Z
```

ACCURATE	DISMALLY	MONOTONY	SCOLDING
ADVISED	DISMISS	MUMMIES	SCOWLED
ALLOTTED	DRIZZLE	MUTUAL	SEEPED
AMASSED	EMERGE	MUZZLED	SHEPHERDED
ASCENDED	EXPOSED	PAUPERS	SHRUNKEN
BAROQUE	IMPOSTER	PEER	SMUG
BROWSING	INJUSTICE	PERSUADE	STAMMERED
CAPER	KEEN	PHARAOH	STEALTHILY
CHAUFFEUR	LIBERTY	PROMPTED	STOWAWAY
CLAMPED	MAIMED	PUBLICITY	SUMMONED
COUNTERED	MASTABA	QUARRIED	TRANSPORTED
DELINQUENT	MATINEE	REGARD	VENDOR
DESCENDING	MEDIOCRE	SARCOPHAGUS	VETO

VOCABULARY WORD SEARCH ANSWER KEY - Mixed Up Files of Mrs. Basil E. Frankweiler

ACCURATE	DISMALLY	MONOTONY	SCOLDING
ADVISED	DISMISS	MUMMIES	SCOWLED
ALLOTTED	DRIZZLE	MUTUAL	SEEPED
AMASSED	EMERGE	MUZZLED	SHEPHERDED
ASCENDED	EXPOSED	PAUPERS	SHRUNKEN
BAROQUE	IMPOSTER	PEER	SMUG
BROWSING	INJUSTICE	PERSUADE	STAMMERED
CAPER	KEEN	PHARAOH	STEALTHILY
CHAUFFEUR	LIBERTY	PROMPTED	STOWAWAY
CLAMPED	MAIMED	PUBLICITY	SUMMONED
COUNTERED	MASTABA	QUARRIED	TRANSPORTED
DELINQUENT	MATINEE	REGARD	VENDOR
DESCENDING	MEDIOCRE	SARCOPHAGUS	VETO

VOCABULARY CROSSWORD - Mixed Up Files of Mrs. Basil E. Frankweiler

Across
1. Collected over time until they form a large fund
3. To rain lightly
7. An afternoon performance of a play, usually with cheaper seats than the evening performance
8. Become used to a certain thing or way of doing things
11. To think of a person or thing in a particular way
13. To look carefully, especially with narrowed eyes
15. Areas of the skin that has been hurt by scraping
17. To exercise the right to reject something
18. To appear
19. A light-hearted adventure or a dangerous illegal activity

Down
2. Shared
4. To make someone very interested
5. A mixture of several unrelated things
6. Slang term for very cool
8. Precise and correct
9. Looking around in a leisurely manner
10. Elaborately or elegantly decorated
12. An ornamental style of European art (mid-16th to early 18th centuries)
14. Revealed
16. Conceited

VOCABULARY CROSSWORD ANSWER KEY - Mixed Up Files of Mrs. Basil E. Frankweiler

			1 A	2 M	A	S	S	E	D		3 D	R	4 I	Z	Z	L	E
				U									N				
				T			5 H		6 K		7 M	A	T	I	N	E	E
		8 A	C	C	U	S	T	O	M	E	D		R				
		C			A		D		E		9 B		I		10 O		
		C			L		G		N		11 R	E	G	A	R	D	
			12 B		13 P	E	E	R			O		U		N		14 E
		U	B		P						W		E		A		X
		15 A	B	R	A	S	16 I	O	N	S		S		D		T		P
		T			O		M		D			I			17 V	E	T	O
		E			Q		U		G			N			L			S
					U		G		18 E	M	E	R	G	E			Y		E
	19 C	A	P	E	R													D

Across
1. Collected over time until they form a large fund
3. To rain lightly
7. An afternoon performance of a play, usually with cheaper seats than the evening performance
8. Become used to a certain thing or way of doing things
11. To think of a person or thing in a particular way
13. To look carefully, especially with narrowed eyes
15. Areas of the skin that has been hurt by scraping
17. To exercise the right to reject something
18. To appear
19. A light-hearted adventure or a dangerous illegal activity

Down
2. Shared
4. To make someone very interested
5. A mixture of several unrelated things
6. Slang term for very cool
8. Precise and correct
9. Looking around in a leisurely manner
10. Elaborately or elegantly decorated
12. An ornamental style of European art (mid-16th to early 18th centuries)
14. Revealed
16. Conceited

VOCABULARY MATCHING 1 - Mixed Up Files of Mrs. Basil E. Frankweiler

___ 1. VETO
___ 2. ASCENDED
___ 3. MONOTONY
___ 4. TYRANNIES
___ 5. INTRIGUED
___ 6. BROWSING
___ 7. ASSOCIATED
___ 8. EXPOSED
___ 9. THEATRICS
___ 10. PUNCTUATED
___ 11. MEDIOCRE
___ 12. ADVISED
___ 13. ABRASIONS
___ 14. COMPLEMENTED
___ 15. SCOLDING
___ 16. AMASSED
___ 17. CAPER
___ 18. STOWAWAY
___ 19. CLAMPED
___ 20. DIRECTED
___ 21. SHUFFLING
___ 22. INJUSTICE
___ 23. PUBLICITY
___ 24. ALLOTTED
___ 25. TRANSPORTED

A. Public interest or knowledge
B. Something completed something else, or made it close to perfect
C. Someone who hides on a traveling vessel in hopes of gaining passage without paying
D. Unfair treatment
E. Display of false and exaggerated emotion
F. To make someone very interested
G. Gave something to somebody as his or her share of what is available
H. Looking around in a leisurely manner
I. Revealed
J. A light-hearted adventure or a dangerous illegal activity
K. Cruelties suffered at the hand of people in authority
L. Held tightly over
M. To end with emphasis
N. Connected to or having to do with
O. Recommended
P. Areas of the skin that has been hurt by scraping
Q. To exercise the right to reject something
R. Collected over time until they form a large fund
S. Complaining, especially when using harsh language
T. boredom that comes from doing the same thing over and over
U. Pointed someone in a particular direction
V. Went upward
W. Moved someone or something from one place to another, especially in a vehicle
X. Adequate, but not very good
Y. To walk without picking up one's feet

VOCABULARY MATCHING 1 ANSWER KEY - Mixed Up Files of Mrs. Basil E. Frankweiler

Q - 1. VETO		A. Public interest or knowledge
V - 2. ASCENDED		B. Something completed something else, or made it close to perfect
T - 3. MONOTONY		C. Someone who hides on a traveling vessel in hopes of gaining passage without paying
K - 4. TYRANNIES		D. Unfair treatment
F - 5. INTRIGUED		E. Display of false and exaggerated emotion
H - 6. BROWSING		F. To make someone very interested
N - 7. ASSOCIATED		G. Gave something to somebody as his or her share of what is available
I - 8. EXPOSED		H. Looking around in a leisurely manner
E - 9. THEATRICS		I. Revealed
M - 10. PUNCTUATED		J. A light-hearted adventure or a dangerous illegal activity
X - 11. MEDIOCRE		K. Cruelties suffered at the hand of people in authority
O - 12. ADVISED		L. Held tightly over
P - 13. ABRASIONS		M. To end with emphasis
B - 14. COMPLEMENTED		N. Connected to or having to do with
S - 15. SCOLDING		O. Recommended
R - 16. AMASSED		P. Areas of the skin that has been hurt by scraping
J - 17. CAPER		Q. To exercise the right to reject something
C - 18. STOWAWAY		R. Collected over time until they form a large fund
L - 19. CLAMPED		S. Complaining, especially when using harsh language
U - 20. DIRECTED		T. boredom that comes from doing the same thing over and over
Y - 21. SHUFFLING		U. Pointed someone in a particular direction
D - 22. INJUSTICE		V. Went upward
A - 23. PUBLICITY		W. Moved someone or something from one place to another, especially in a vehicle
G - 24. ALLOTTED		X. Adequate, but not very good
W 25. TRANSPORTED		Y. To walk without picking up one's feet

VOCABULARY MATCHING 2 - Mixed Up Files of Mrs. Basil E. Frankweiler

___ 1. SHUFFLING   A. Affected with a severe and permanent injury

___ 2. SHRUNKEN   B. To rain lightly

___ 3. LIBERTY   C. Looking around in a leisurely manner

___ 4. COMPLEMENTED   D. An explanation at the bottom of a page giving further information about something in the text above

___ 5. MUMMIES   E. Revealing or telling about

___ 6. DRIZZLE   F. Adequate, but not very good

___ 7. STAMMERED   G. Noisy activity or confusion

___ 8. DISMALLY   H. Bodies of people that have been embalmed and wrapped in cloth, as was the custom in ancient Egypt

___ 9. BROWSING   I. Areas of the skin that has been hurt by scraping

___10. COMMOTION   J. Precise and correct

___11. FOOTNOTES   K. To end with emphasis

___12. PUNCTUATED   L. Spoke with many hesitations due to fear or strong emotion

___13. CHAUFFEUR   M. Something completed something else, or made it close to perfect

___14. ACCURATE   N. In a depressing manner

___15. STEALTHILY   O. A feeling of modesty

___16. PUBLICITY   P. Freedom to think or act

___17. MONOTONY   Q. Public interest or knowledge

___18. KEEN   R. Characterized by a decrease in size

___19. MEDIOCRE   S. A light-hearted adventure or a dangerous illegal activity

___20. MAIMED   T. Slang term for very cool

___21. DISCLOSING   U. boredom that comes from doing the same thing over and over

___22. ORNATELY   V. Driver

___23. CAPER   W. Elaborately or elegantly decorated

___24. ABRASIONS   X. Secretively or cunningly

___25. HUMILITY   Y. To walk without picking up one's feet

VOCABULARY MATCHING 2 ANSWER KEY - Mixed Up Files of Mrs. Basil E. Frankweiler

Y - 1.	SHUFFLING	A. Affected with a severe and permanent injury
R - 2.	SHRUNKEN	B. To rain lightly
P - 3.	LIBERTY	C. Looking around in a leisurely manner
M - 4.	COMPLEMENTED	D. An explanation at the bottom of a page giving further information about something in the text above
H - 5.	MUMMIES	E. Revealing or telling about
B - 6.	DRIZZLE	F. Adequate, but not very good
L - 7.	STAMMERED	G. Noisy activity or confusion
N - 8.	DISMALLY	H. Bodies of people that have been embalmed and wrapped in cloth, as was the custom in ancient Egypt
C - 9.	BROWSING	I. Areas of the skin that has been hurt by scraping
G -10.	COMMOTION	J. Precise and correct
D -11.	FOOTNOTES	K. To end with emphasis
K -12.	PUNCTUATED	L. Spoke with many hesitations due to fear or strong emotion
V -13.	CHAUFFEUR	M. Something completed something else, or made it close to perfect
J - 14.	ACCURATE	N. In a depressing manner
X -15.	STEALTHILY	O. A feeling of modesty
Q -16.	PUBLICITY	P. Freedom to think or act
U -17.	MONOTONY	Q. Public interest or knowledge
T -18.	KEEN	R. Characterized by a decrease in size
F -19.	MEDIOCRE	S. A light-hearted adventure or a dangerous illegal activity
A -20.	MAIMED	T. Slang term for very cool
E -21.	DISCLOSING	U. boredom that comes from doing the same thing over and over
W 22.	ORNATELY	V. Driver
S -23.	CAPER	W. Elaborately or elegantly decorated
I - 24.	ABRASIONS	X. Secretively or cunningly
O -25.	HUMILITY	Y. To walk without picking up one's feet

VOCABULARY JUGGLE LETTER 1 - Mixed Up Files of Mrs. Basil E. Frankweiler

1. TETPNAUCUD = 1. _____
   To end with emphasis

2. HSHEDEDPRE = 2. _____
   Guided a group of people or animals

3. EACNSDDE = 3. _____
   Went upward

4. GDEECDNSNI = 4. _____
   Coming down

5. AAITSECODS = 5. _____
   Connected to or having to do with

6. ELNYARTO = 6. _____
   Elaborately or elegantly decorated

7. UPAREPS = 7. _____
   Extremely poor individuals

8. AUMULT = 8. _____
   Shared

9. DEUSAPER = 9. _____
   To convince or make someone believe something

10. TALEFTYR = 10. _____
    The act of complimenting someone for the purpose of getting something

11. TOUEADCMCS = 11. _____
    Become used to a certain thing or way of doing things

12. TABASAM = 12. _____
    An ancient Egyptian tomb with a flat base, sloping sides, and a flat roof

13. TCREEDID = 13. _____
    Pointed someone in a particular direction

14. IRLTEYB = 14. _____
    Freedom to think or act

15. EMOICRDE =15. _____
Adequate, but not very good

16. ISMMEMU =16. _____
Bodies of people that have been embalmed and wrapped in cloth, as was the custom in ancient Egypt

17. REPE =17. _____
To look carefully, especially with narrowed eyes

18. NGUITBIRTAT =18. _____
Giving credit to a person for a particular piece of art or work of literature

19. AILMLDSY =19. _____
In a depressing manner

20. RDERAG =20. _____
To think of a person or thing in a particular way

21. ITHYIULM =21. _____
A feeling of modesty

22. PSROEITM =22. _____
Someone who pretends to be someone he is not

23. SARYTNIEN =23. _____
Cruelties suffered at the hand of people in authority

24. ATWYAOWS =24. _____
Someone who hides on a traveling vessel in hopes of gaining passage without paying

25. IEDNETLQNU =25. _____
A young person who has broken the law

26. ISSISMD =26. _____
To officially release students from school

27. THISLAETYL =27. _____
Secretively or cunningly

28. ETNIAEM =28. _____
An afternoon performance of a play, usually with cheaper seats than the evening performance

29. NEKE =29. _____
Slang term for very cool

30. DLEOCSW =30. _____
Made a facial expression characterized by drawing the eyebrows together in anger or displeasure

31. VDEAIDS =31. _____
Recommended

32. UTRDOEECN =32. _____
To say something that contradicts what someone else has said

33. ESMTDAERM =33. _____
Spoke with many hesitations due to fear or strong emotion

34. EALDPCM =34. _____
Held tightly over

35. ONNOTOYM =35. _____
boredom that comes from doing the same thing over and over

36. NCDSIOILSG =36. _____
Revealing or telling about

37. ODPEPMTR =37. _____
Urged

38. ELIZDZR =38. _____
To rain lightly

VOCABULARY JUGGLE LETTER 1 ANSWER KEY - Mixed Up Files of Mrs. Basil E. Frankweiler

1. TETPNAUCUD = 1. PUNCTUATED
To end with emphasis

2. HSHEDEDPRE = 2. SHEPHERDED
Guided a group of people or animals

3. EACNSDDE = 3. ASCENDED
Went upward

4. GDEECDNSNI = 4. DESCENDING
Coming down

5. AAITSECODS = 5. ASSOCIATED
Connected to or having to do with

6. ELNYARTO = 6. ORNATELY
Elaborately or elegantly decorated

7. UPAREPS = 7. PAUPERS
Extremely poor individuals

8. AUMULT = 8. MUTUAL
Shared

9. DEUSAPER = 9. PERSUADE
To convince or make someone believe something

10. TALEFTYR = 10. FLATTERY
The act of complimenting someone for the purpose of getting something

11. TOUEADCMCS = 11. ACCUSTOMED
Become used to a certain thing or way of doing things

12. TABASAM = 12. MASTABA
An ancient Egyptian tomb with a flat base, sloping sides, and a flat roof

13. TCREEDID = 13. DIRECTED
Pointed someone in a particular direction

14. IRLTEYB = 14. LIBERTY
Freedom to think or act

15. EMOICRDE =15. MEDIOCRE

Adequate, but not very good

16. ISMMEMU =16. MUMMIES

Bodies of people that have been embalmed and wrapped in cloth, as was the custom in ancient Egypt

17. REPE =17. PEER

To look carefully, especially with narrowed eyes

18. NGUITBIRTAT =18. ATTRIBUTING

Giving credit to a person for a particular piece of art or work of literature

19. AILMLDSY =19. DISMALLY

In a depressing manner

20. RDERAG =20. REGARD

To think of a person or thing in a particular way

21. ITHYIULM =21. HUMILITY

A feeling of modesty

22. PSROEITM =22. IMPOSTER

Someone who pretends to be someone he is not

23. SARYTNIEN =23. TYRANNIES

Cruelties suffered at the hand of people in authority

24. ATWYAOWS =24. STOWAWAY

Someone who hides on a traveling vessel in hopes of gaining passage without paying

25. IEDNETLQNU =25. DELINQUENT

A young person who has broken the law

26. ISSISMD =26. DISMISS

To officially release students from school

27. THISLAETYL =27. STEALTHILY

Secretively or cunningly

28. ETNIAEM =28. MATINEE

An afternoon performance of a play, usually with cheaper seats than the evening performance

29. NEKE =29. KEEN

Slang term for very cool

30. DLEOCSW =30. SCOWLED
Made a facial expression characterized by drawing the eyebrows together in anger or displeasure

31. VDEAIDS =31. ADVISED
Recommended

32. UTRDOEECN =32. COUNTERED
To say something that contradicts what someone else has said

33. ESMTDAERM =33. STAMMERED
Spoke with many hesitations due to fear or strong emotion

34. EALDPCM =34. CLAMPED
Held tightly over

35. ONNOTOYM =35. MONOTONY
boredom that comes from doing the same thing over and over

36. NCDSIOILSG =36. DISCLOSING
Revealing or telling about

37. ODPEPMTR =37. PROMPTED
Urged

38. ELIZDZR =38. DRIZZLE
To rain lightly

VOCABULARY JUGGLE LETTER 2 - Mixed Up Files of Mrs. Basil E. Frankweiler

1. ILCTPBUYI = 1. _____
   Public interest or knowledge

2. NUNRSEHK = 2. _____
   Characterized by a decrease in size

3. TESOOOTFN = 3. _____
   An explanation at the bottom of a page giving further information about something in the text above

4. GMSU = 4. _____
   Conceited

5. EDZZLMU = 5. _____
   Prevented a person from speaking, especially in public

6. ISGNROBW = 6. _____
   Looking around in a leisurely manner

7. TEOV = 7. _____
   To exercise the right to reject something

8. FEUHFUACR = 8. _____
   Driver

9. EPDSEE = 9. _____
   Passed through an opening very slowly

10. CECRSEEHD = 10. _____
    Made a loud, high-pitched sound

11. ETDLTOAL = 11. _____
    Gave something to somebody as his or her share of what is available

12. EMEEGR = 12. _____
    To appear

13. STEADOPRRNT = 13. _____
    Moved someone or something from one place to another, especially in a vehicle

14. DRUIPOEPCCE =14. _____
Totally absorbed in doing or thinking about something else

15. CUARTEAC =15. _____
Precise and correct

16. QORUEAB =16. _____
An ornamental style of European art (mid-16th to early 18th centuries)

17. PCAER =17. _____
A light-hearted adventure or a dangerous illegal activity

18. GUFNFISHL =18. _____
To walk without picking up one's feet

19. NCEIUTJSI =19. _____
Unfair treatment

20. DNRVEO =20. _____
Someone who sells something

21. ODSXEPE =21. _____
Revealed

22. CAHUPAOSSRG =22. _____
An ancient stone or marble coffin

23. THCAESIRT =23. _____
Display of false and exaggerated emotion

24. OOTICNOMM =24. _____
Noisy activity or confusion

25. EDGGPDOHEO =25. _____
A mixture of several unrelated things

26. LCDTMEOEPMNE =26. _____
Something completed something else, or made it close to perfect

27. MDMIAE =27. _____
Affected with a severe and permanent injury

28. OIDLSCGN =28. _____
Complaining, especially when using harsh language

29. SAEDEEDC =29. _____
Dead

30. RQDUREAI =30. _____
Obtained or gotten after much effort

31. RAHOAPH =31. _____
A king of ancient Egypt

32. EETECUTRIOFDN =32. _____
Made a realistic copy of

33. EGRIITNUD =33. _____
To make someone very interested

34. NRAASBISO =34. _____
Areas of the skin that has been hurt by scraping

35. UDESNOMM =35. _____
Sent for someone to come

36. TPHOCEIROD =36. _____
Relating to disorders of the bones, joints, ligaments, or muscles

37. DMASEAS =37. _____
Collected over time until they form a large fund

VOCABULARY JUGGLE LETTER 2 ANSWER KEY - Mixed Up Files of Mrs. Basil E. Frankweiler

1. ILCTPBUYI = 1. PUBLICITY

    Public interest or knowledge

2. NUNRSEHK = 2. SHRUNKEN

    Characterized by a decrease in size

3. TESOOOTFN = 3. FOOTNOTES

    An explanation at the bottom of a page giving further information about something in the text above

4. GMSU = 4. SMUG

    Conceited

5. EDZZLMU = 5. MUZZLED

    Prevented a person from speaking, especially in public

6. ISGNROBW = 6. BROWSING

    Looking around in a leisurely manner

7. TEOV = 7. VETO

    To exercise the right to reject something

8. FEUHFUACR = 8. CHAUFFEUR

    Driver

9. EPDSEE = 9. SEEPED

    Passed through an opening very slowly

10. CECRSEEHD =10. SCREECHED

    Made a loud, high-pitched sound

11. ETDLTOAL =11. ALLOTTED

    Gave something to somebody as his or her share of what is available

12. EMEEGR =12. EMERGE

    To appear

13. STEADOPRRNT =13. TRANSPORTED

    Moved someone or something from one place to another, especially in a vehicle

14. DRUIPOEPCCE =14. PREOCCUPIED
Totally absorbed in doing or thinking about something else

15. CUARTEAC =15. ACCURATE
Precise and correct

16. QORUEAB =16. BAROQUE
An ornamental style of European art (mid-16th to early 18th centuries)

17. PCAER =17. CAPER
A light-hearted adventure or a dangerous illegal activity

18. GUFNFISHL =18. SHUFFLING
To walk without picking up one's feet

19. NCEIUTJSI =19. INJUSTICE
Unfair treatment

20. DNRVEO =20. VENDOR
Someone who sells something

21. ODSXEPE =21. EXPOSED
Revealed

22. CAHUPAOSSRG =22. SARCOPHAGUS
An ancient stone or marble coffin

23. THCAESIRT =23. THEATRICS
Display of false and exaggerated emotion

24. OOTICNOMM =24. COMMOTION
Noisy activity or confusion

25. EDGGPDOHEO =25. HODGEPODGE
A mixture of several unrelated things

26. LCDTMEOEPMNE =26. COMPLEMENTED
Something completed something else, or made it close to perfect

27. MDMIAE =27. MAIMED
Affected with a severe and permanent injury

28. OIDLSCGN =28. SCOLDING
Complaining, especially when using harsh language

29. SAEDEEDC =29. DECEASED
Dead

30. RQDUREAI =30. QUARRIED
Obtained or gotten after much effort

31. RAHOAPH =31. PHARAOH
A king of ancient Egypt

32. EETECUTRIOFDN =32. COUNTERFEITED
Made a realistic copy of

33. EGRIITNUD =33. INTRIGUED
To make someone very interested

34. NRAASBISO =34. ABRASIONS
Areas of the skin that has been hurt by scraping

35. UDESNOMM =35. SUMMONED
Sent for someone to come

36. TPHOCEIROD =36. ORTHOPEDIC
Relating to disorders of the bones, joints, ligaments, or muscles

37. DMASEAS =37. AMASSED
Collected over time until they form a large fund

www.ingramcontent.com/pod-product-compliance
Lightning Source LLC
LaVergne TN
LVHW081533060526
838200LV00048B/2071